HITLER'S
ATLANTIC WALL

FROM SOUTHERN FRANCE TO NORTHERN NORWAY, YESTERDAY AND TODAY

HITLER'S ATLANTIC WALL

FROM SOUTHERN FRANCE TO NORTHERN NORWAY, YESTERDAY AND TODAY

George Forty, Leo Marriott and Simon Forty

Published in the United States of America and Great Britain in 2016 by
CASEMATE PUBLISHERS
1950 Lawrence Road, Havertown, PA 19083
and
10 Hythe Bridge Street, Oxford, OX1 2EW

ISBN-13: 978-1-61200-375-7

Produced by Greene Media Ltd., 34 Dean Street, Brighton BN1 3EG

Cataloging-in-publication data is available from the Library of Congress and the British Library.

10 9 8 7 6 5 4 3 2 1

Printed and bound in China

For a complete list of Casemate titles please contact:

CASEMATE PUBLISHERS (US)
Telephone (610) 853-9131, Fax (610) 853-9146
E-mail: casemate@casematepublishing.com

CASEMATE PUBLISHERS (UK)
Telephone (01865) 241249, Fax (01865) 794449
E-mail: casemate-uk@casematepublishing.co.uk

Abbreviations & Glossary

AA/AAA anti-aircraft (artillery)
Abt *Abteilung*
ArGr/ArUGr/ArOGr Artillery group; Artillery under group/over group
Captured gun identifiers: *Austria (ö), Belgium (b), Czech (t), England (e), France (f), Holland (h), Norway (n), Poland (p), Soviet (r), Yugoslavia (j).*
CP command post
FA field artillery
FdU West = *Führer der U-Boote im Westraum* = OC U-boats in the west (France)
Festung fortress
FJR *Fallschirmjäger* = paratrooper
Flak *Flugzeugabwehrkanone* = AAA
FuM *Funkmess* = radar
FuMO = *FuM-Ortung* = radar direction finder, active ranging
FuMB = *FuM-Beobachtung* = radar detector, passive detection
FuME = *FuM-Erkennung* = radar detector, active IFF
FuMS = *FuM-Störsender* = radar interference sender, active jamming
FuMT = *FuM-Täuschung* = radar deceptor, active deception
FuMZ = *FuM-Zusatz* = radar with specialized improvements
GR *Grenadier Regt*
HKAA/R *Heeres Küstenartillerie Abt/Regt*
HKB *Heeres Küsten Batterie* = army coastal bty
ID *Infanterie-Division*
IFF Identification Friend/Foe
Ingenieur civil engineer
KwK *Kampfwagenkanone* = tank gun
Leitstand fire-direction center
m *mittlere* = medium
MAA/R *Marine Artillerie Abt/Regt*
MFlB *Marine Flak Batterie* = naval AA bty
MKB *Marine Küsten Batterie* = naval coastal bty
MP = *Marinepeilstand* = Naval direction-finding tower
MSB *Marine Seeziel Batterie* = Naval bty tasked with targets at sea
OB West *Oberbefehlshaber West* = C-in-C West

OKH/L/M *Oberkommando des Heeres/der Luftwaffe/der Marine* = Army/Airforce/Navy High Command
OT *Organisation Todt*
PaK *Panzerabwehrkanone* = ATk gun
Panzermauer *Panzerabwehrkanone*
PzGr *Panzergrenadier* = armored infantry
RAD *Reichsarbeitsdienst* = State Labour Service
RAD/M *RAD Mann/Männer* = Men's RAD
RAD/wJ *RAD der weiblichen Jugend* = RAD for young women
Pionier military engineer
Regelbau prefixes:
R   *Heer*   Army
M   *Kriegsmarine*   Navy
S   *Kriegsmarine*   Navy heavy
Fl   *Kriegsmarine Flak*   Navy AA
L   *Luftwaffe*   Airforce
S-mine *Schuh-mine* = anti-personnel mine
SdKfz *Sonderkraftfahrzeug* = special purpose vehicle
SEEKO–KI *Kriegsmarine* C-in-C Channel Islands
Seezielbatterie see MSB
SK either *Sonderkonstruktion* (special, not *Regelbau*, build) or *Schnelladekanone* (quick-loading as in guns)
***Sperrbatterie* (SPB)** = lit: blocking bty—a bty placed to block an entrance (eg a harbour entrance)
sPzAbt *Schwere Panzer-Abteilung* = heavy tank detachment
STO *Service Travail Obligatoire* = (French) compulsory work service
StP *Stützpunkt* = strongpoint
StPGr *Stützpunktgruppe* = group of strongpoints
StuG *Sturmgeschütz* = assault gun
TT torpedo tube
USAAF US Army Air Force
V *Versorgung* = support
VB *Verteidigungsbereich* = defense area
Vf *verstärkt feldmäßig* = strengthened to withstand 10.5cm shells or 12cm mortars
WN *Widerstandsnest* = pocket of resistance

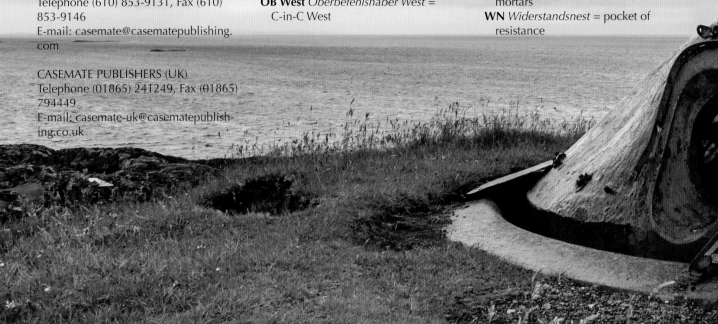

CONTENTS

INTRODUCTION

He who defends everything defends nothing. Frederick the Great's famous maxim rings loud in every discussion of the Atlantic Wall. If one discounts the 'Iron Curtain' of the Cold War, the Atlantic Wall was the last great static defensive line to be built in Europe. However, unlike its closest predecessors, the Maginot and Siegfried lines, its enormous length—over 5,000km (3,125 plus miles) stretching from Norway's northern tip to the Spanish/French border—the vast range of different types of fortifications produced; the massive workforce employed; the incredible amount of concrete, steel and other materials used; and finally, the length of time it took to build (1940–44), all make it unique among European defensive lines.

The fact that so much of it remains is a somber testament to the way it was built: no expense was spared because the materials and workforce were primarily from the occupied countries—initially, some paid workmen but in the main many slave labourers, all forced to work for the Nazis. The intention was to create a continuous wall that would stand up to an enemy invasion anywhere along the coastline of northwest Europe (and later, partly along the Mediterranean as well), to defend Nazi European gains from inevitable attack. I say inevitable: while there is a very good argument that the resources of Britain and its Commonwealth would also have led to an offensive in time, the attack on America by Japan and Germany's declaration of war made it certain. Once US resources were committed wholesale, the Nazi demise was merely a question of time.

Operation 'Sealion'

When did the Nazi mindset turn from attack to defence? There was no single underlying event that led to the initial building of major defences along the western European coast. In 1940, after the fall of France and the Low Countries, Britain showed no signs of surrendering. Planning for Operation *Seelöwe* ('Sealion'), the amphibious invasion of England, was outlined in Hitler's Directive 16, 'On preparations for a landing operation against England', issued 16 July 1940. This included the installation of four heavy naval batteries in the Calais–Boulogne area—not to defend the coast, but rather to back up the intended invasion. This is confirmed in a treatise on the Organisation Todt (OT), written postwar by Franz Xaver Dorsch, Deputy Chief of the OT, in which he says:

'The first, rather large, combined work of the OT after the construction of the Westwall was the installation of the heavy batteries at Cap Gris-Nez. According to an official announcement of the Naval Warfare Command, this work was part of Operation Sealion. It was supposed to have provided the necessary fire support to the units that were committed for a landing operation in England. It should not go unmentioned at this point Hitler declared, when inspecting the batteries on 23 December 1940, that he never gave serious thought to Operation Sealion. The value of the batteries, even without taking "Sealion" into consideration, was no doubt afforded by the fact that a blocking of the Channel, up to a certain degree, for enemy ships was thereby given support.

'The naval commandant (Admiral Fischer) personally took it upon himself to designate the locations of the batteries. The construction work itself was under the OT-Einsatzstab on the Channel coast in Audinghen, which I personally directed.'

The first OT workers were housed in a former British Army camp near Étaples, some 15km southwest of Boulogne, 'a corrugated iron barracks in which most of the workers who had been quickly assembled could be given shelter at once.' In fact in Directive 16, Hitler gave his approval for this action when he said:

'The largest possible number of extra-heavy guns will be brought into position as soon as possible in order to cover the crossing (to support "Sealion") and to shield the flanks against enemy action at sea. For this purpose railway guns will also be used (reinforced by all available captured weapons) and will be sited on railway turntables. Those batteries intended only to deal with targets on the English mainland (K5 and K12) will not be included. Apart from this the existing extra-heavy platform-gun batteries are to be enclosed in concrete opposite the Strait of Dover within the limits of their range. The technical work will be the responsibility of the Organisation Todt.'

Even when 'Sealion' was postponed indefinitely, no formal order was immediately given for the systematic building of defences anywhere along the coast, but rather major construction effort was given over to the building of submarine pens in places like Brest, Lorient and St Nazaire.

As part of the 'Sealion' operation, both the OKW and Hitler fully appreciated the need to blockade the Strait of Dover and considered the task perfectly possible, because only 21 miles of sea separated the two coastlines. In his book *Invasion of England 1940*, Peter Schenk explains that the issue of the use of coastal batteries was brought up on 15 July 1940 at a meeting with Hitler at the Berghof, when it was agreed that every available piece of heavy artillery would be set up in suitable selected positions along the Channel coast to support 'Sealion'. The Kriegsmarine reckoned that it would take at least three months for this work to be completed and the Organisation Todt was given the task of carrying it out. They began on 22 July 1940. To quote Peter Schenk:

'The battery Grosser Kurfürst at Pillau [in Prussia; today's Baltiysk] was dismantled and re-erected at the Pas de Calais, where three guns were ready to fire by 31 July. At the beginning of August, the four 28cm traversing turrets of this battery were fully operational, as were all the Heer's railway guns. The latter comprised six 28cm K5 guns in two batteries and a 21cm K12 gun with a range of 115km. These two types were only for land bombardment while the other railway guns could be used against maritime targets. These were the eight 28cm Kurze Bruno in two batteries; two 28cm Schwere Bruno; three 28cm Lange Bruno, the latter of which were set up at Cherbourg. Six 24cm K3 guns (motorised), six Czech 24cm guns (motorised) and 10 21cm K39 guns (motorised) were also erected at the Pas de Calais. These too were only limited use against naval targets. The Heer guns were placed under Kriegsmarine command to ensure uniform fire.'

By mid-August three more heavy naval batteries had become operational: Friedrich August (3 x 30.5cm guns), Prinz Heinrich (2 x 28cm guns) and Oldenburg (2 x 24cm guns). Two other batteries—Hamburg and York (both 24cm guns)—were also installed on the Cherbourg peninsula. Finally, in September, Siegfried (2 x 38cm guns) was ready. This last battery would later

This NASA photograph, taken in April 2003, although slightly obscured by Saharan sand (the brown patches) shows well the proximity of Great Britain to the European coastline. Jacques Descloitres, MODIS Rapid Response Team, NASA/GSFC

Page 1: *Azeville on the Cherbourg peninsula after capture. NARA*

Page 2–3: *Battery Oldenburg, part of the German offensive capability at "Hellfire Corner" the closest point between France and the UK.*

Page 4–5: *Operation 'Checkmate' was a Commando raid that sank a minesweeper in Haugesund harbour, Norway in 1942. This 7.5cm Belgian-made gun turret is one of four in two sections of HKB 68./977 placed to protect the harbour later in 1942. Petr Podebradsky*

be renamed Todt in honour of the work done by Fritz Todt's organisation. In addition to these heavy batteries, the Heer and Kriegsmarine together deployed some 444 medium and light guns in batteries along the Dutch, Belgian and French coastlines, their main task being to protect coastal shipping routes and ports/harbours. As well as the guns, some fire control radars were installed, to work with the heavy batteries at Blanc Nez, Cap d'Alprech, Cap de Hague and Cap d'Antifer (near Le Havre).

While not identified as such, in reality this was the first phase of construction of the Atlantic Wall. Elsewhere, taking Belgium as an example, the ports of Blankenberge, Zeebrugge, Oostende and Nieuwpoort, despite the fact that they were at that time all less important than the large French coastal ports, soon also became protected by naval and army batteries.

Although 'Sealion' was postponed in autumn of 1940, an earlier operation—'Green Arrow' (*Grüner Pfeil*) had already taken place, namely the relatively peaceful occupation of the British Channel Islands by German forces, 30 June–3 July 1940. The Channel Islands became a special place as far as Hitler was concerned. He rated them so important as to station there the largest infantry division in the Heer. The only part of the British Isles to be occupied by the Germans, some of the fortifications built on the Channel Islands were unique within the Atlantic Wall. The islanders would have to put up with five long years of occupation until they were liberated on 9 May 1945, with the German surrender and the arrival of British troops.

The Second Front

At this moment, victorious in east and west, Hitler's lust for *Lebensraum* overtook him. The search for expansion space in the east wasn't his idea: Germans had been eyeing the east since the Middle Ages, but he was the first German leader to be able to put theory into practice. On 18 December 1940 his Directive 21 identified his intentions. These came to fruition on 22 June 1941 when Operation 'Barbarossa' unleashed German forces on Russia. As the German penetrations extended closer and closer to the outskirts of Moscow itself, the Russians demanded their allies opened a Second Front in the west on the mainland of Europe in order to divert pressure from the hard-pressed Red Army. By mid-1942, as the Germans hammered against Stalingrad, both Stalin and the United States pressed for a Second Front.

For a variety of reasons—mainly the lack of suitable equipment and the opposition of Winston Churchill, cautious about incurring a dramatic defeat

Today, one of the huge Todt Battery casemates is a museum. Alongside is a Krupp K5 railway gun of the type used against England. With little or no traverse it had to be sighted by moving it on a section of curved track. It could propel a 562lb shell some 40 miles at a firing rate of one every four minutes. During the war, bombardment of the English coast would damage 10,000 buildings and kill over 200 people, although its effects on shipping were less notable.

just as the tide turned—a cross-Channel invasion was put back. The experience of the Dieppe Raid (19 August 1942) furthered that view; more successful operations on the African coast (8 November 1942), Sicily (6 July 1943), Salerno (3 September 1943), and Anzio (22 January 1944), as well as those in the Pacific, showed the Allies the way and also gave time for specialised equipment to be designed and manufactured.

For the Allies the drawback to these decisions was that the defenders had time to prepare. Already on 14 December 1941 the OKW had issued a directive detailing the building of a 'new Westwall'. It was issued with Hitler's full approval, but actually signed by Generalfeldmarschall Wilhelm Keitel (Chief of Staff of OKW) and its opening paragraph set out the concept thus:

'The coastal regions of the Arctic Ocean, North Sea and Atlantic Ocean which we control are ultimately to be built into a "Neue Westwall" in order that we can be sure of repelling any landing attempt, however strong, using the smallest possible number of permanently stationed troops.'

Heads down in prayer, Churchill and Roosevelt personnified the 'special relationship' between the two countries in World War II. Their cordiality, however, masked disagreements about when the invasion should take place.

The directive went on to explain that the aim was to construct a series of coastal batteries to ensure long-range coastal defence. In addition, it explained that it had been decided to build bunkers of the *verstärkt feldmäßig* (Vf) type, that is to say, reinforced field fortifications that were different from the ordinary, usually temporary, field fortifications (made of earth, wood and masonry). The Vf type would be built of masonry or reinforced concrete with ceilings and walls between 0.30m and 1.5m thick. In view of the fact that at that time there was little enemy air activity, open, circular gun emplacements were chosen. With the construction of the 'New Westwall' all the existing coastal artillery batteries were to be improved and extra protection from *Stützpunkte* (strongpoints) would be given to coastal areas considered to be under threat.

Priorities were given for the construction in certain specific areas. Norway was given top priority: first, because it was difficult to use mobile reserves there; then because of the terrain and weather; and finally, because there was an urgent need to increase the number of harbour defences available to protect coastal shipping. Belgium and France's western coasts were then given second priority, with the open coasts of the Netherlands and Jutland third. Most of the construction of these coastal defences would be under Heer control, but the Kriegsmarine was made responsible for Norway and for all measures which involved sea warfare. Air defence was naturally put under the Luftwaffe, whilst the actual construction work in all areas was to be handled by the Organisation Todt.

As the war intensified in 1942, the OKW was forced to send more and more reinforcements to other areas—mainly the Mediterranean and the Eastern Front—so the defences in the west were inevitably weakened. This danger was appreciated by Hitler and the OKW and gave rise to a plan for the defence of western coasts enshrined in the *Küstenverteidigung* (coastal defence) Directive 40 of 23 March 1942 (see below).

An additional reason for the directive was the operations of the newly formed British commandos. Their early raids were unsuccessful but on 4 March 1941 they attacked the Lofoten Islands in northern Norway destroying factories producing glycerine. This was followed on 26 December by another raid on the Lofoten Islands designed to divert German attention during a further commando raid—the bloody encounter at Vaagso (Vågsøy) on 27 December 1941. This small-scale operation (Operation 'Archery') against the German-occupied islands at the entrance to Nordfjord was designed to prevent German troops from being moved from Norway and sent to the Eastern Front. German military installations were wrecked and the supporting RN ships neutralised several of the nearby shore batteries.

Finally, as if to underline the need for Directive 40, a few days after it was released St Nazaire was attacked on the night of 28–29 March 1942. Operation 'Chariot' saw the Normandie drydock destroyed by Commandos. The price was high: 169 dead and 215 captured but the drydock was destroyed thus helping to keep *Tirpitz* in northern waters.

Directive 40

The directive (at right) was issued by the Führer's Headquarters on 23 March 1942, under the title: 'Competence of Commanders in Coastal Areas'. While it reiterated much of what had been said in Keitel's earlier directive of the previous December, it clearly was the starting point from which the Atlantic Wall proper was conceived. Although it attempted to produce a set of rules that could not be misinterpreted, human nature and inter-service rivalry soon led to differences of opinion, some fundamental.

Below Hitler and the OKW, instead of one supreme commander as was to be the case on the Allied side, the *Oberbefehlshaber West* (OBW), Feldmarschall Gerd von Rundstedt, was purely a land commander, having no direct control over any sea or air forces. The senior admiral (Theodor Krancke who commanded Marinegruppe West) still received his orders direct from Oberkommando der Marine (OKM—Navy High Command), while the senior Luftwaffe general (Feldmarschall Hugo Sperrle who commanded Luftflotte 3) received his orders direct from the Oberkommando der Luftwaffe (OKL). As Rommel's chief of staff, Hans Speidel, wryly commented in his book *We Defended Normandy*:

'Operations at sea and in the air could thus be co-ordinated neither by the C-in-C West nor by the Army Group commander. The military commanders were only partially informed of the intentions of the other two services and usually too late.'

In any case von Rundstedt, who had gone into voluntary retirement at the

The British Commando raids were pinpricks, but they had the desired effect of leading to a German response out of all proportion to their size and importance. As well as the notorious Commando Order of 18 October 1942 (that all Allied commandos should be executed when captured even if in uniform), the defensive structures and manpower tied up to defend against such attacks kept many troops away from front lines.

DIRECTIVE 40

I. General Considerations

1. In the coming months, the coastline of Europe will be vulnerable to the danger of an enemy landing in strength. The time and place of such landing operations may not be dictated by operational considerations only. For example, setbacks in other areas, obligations to Allies and political considerations, may persuade him to take action which might appear unlikely from a purely military point of view.

2. Even enemy landing operations which have limited objectives could have serious repercussions on our own plans if they result in the enemy gaining a foothold on the coast. Our coastal sea traffic could be interrupted and they may pin down significant numbers of our Heer and Luftwaffe in dealing with them, which may require them to be withdrawn from other important areas. Capturing one of our airfields or establishing a bridgehead would be particularly dangerous.

3. There are many important military and industrial locations all along the coastline or close by, some of which are equipped with especially valuable plant, which may tempt the enemy into making surprise local attacks.

4. Particular attention must be made to preparations in England for amphibious landings on open coastline, because they have at their disposal numerous armoured landing craft, able to carry armoured fighting vehicles and heavy weapons. The possibility of parachute and airborne attacks on a large scale must also be considered.

II. General Operational Instructions for Coastal Defence

1. Coastal defence is a task for everyone and calls for especially close and complete co-operation between all units of the three services.

2. In addition to naval and air reconnaissance, the intelligence service must endeavour to obtain early information on the state of enemy readiness and their preparations for any amphibious landing operation. All suitable air and sea units will then concentrate on attacking enemy embarkation locations and their convoys, so as to defeat and destroy them as far from our coast as possible. However, it may be that by clever camouflage and/or taking advantage of bad weather conditions, the enemy may achieve a surprise attack. All troops who may be exposed to such surprise attacks must be at a state of permanent readiness. One of the most important duties of commanding officers of such units must be to overcome a lack of vigilance among their troops which, as experience has shown, is bound to increase as time passes.

3. As recent battle experience has shown, the responsibility for planning and implementation of all defensive matters formulated in the defence of the coast—including coastal waters within range of medium coastal artillery—must lie unequivocally and unreservedly in the hands of a single commander. This commander must be able to make use of all available forces and weapons of all branches of the Wehrmacht, of organisations and units outside the armed forces, and of our civilian headquarters in the area, for the sole purpose of destroying enemy transports and landing forces. He will use them so that the attack collapses, if possible, before it reaches the coast, or at the latest, on the coast itself. Enemy forces that do manage to land must be destroyed or thrown back into the sea by an immediate counter-attack. Everyone carrying weapons, no matter what branch of service or non-service organisation they belong to, must do this. Additionally, the working of the naval shore establishments must be guaranteed, in so far as they are not themselves involved in the fighting on land. This applies equally to Luftwaffe ground staff and anti-aircraft defence of airfields. No headquarters is to initiate a withdrawal in such circumstances. All German troops stationed on or near the coast must be armed and trained for battle. The enemy must also be prevented from securing a foothold on any islands that present a threat to the mainland or to coastal shipping.

4. The distribution of forces and the building of defensive works must be carried out so that our strongest defence positions are located in those sectors most likely to be selected by the enemy for landings (fortified areas). Other coastal sectors that may be threatened by small-scale surprise attacks will be defended by a series of strongpoints, supported, where possible, by the coastal batteries. Important military and industrial plant will be included within these strongpoints. The same principles will apply to offshore islands, whilst less-threatened areas will be kept under observation.

5. The coast will be divided into sectors as decided by the three services in mutual agreement or, should the situation demand it, by the responsible commander [see Para III-1 below] whose decision will be final.

6. The fortified areas and strongpoints must be able, by virtue of proper distribution of forces, completion of all-round defence and by their supply situation, to hold out for some time even against a superior enemy force. Fortified areas and strongpoints will be defended to the last man. They must never be forced to surrender from lack of ammunition, rations or water.

7. The responsible commanders [see Para III-2 below] will issue orders for keeping the coast under constant observation and will ensure that reconnaissance reports from all three services are quickly evaluated, co-ordinated and sent to the headquarters and civilian authorities concerned. As soon as there is any evidence that an enemy operation is imminent, then the commander is authorised to issue the necessary instructions for co-ordinated and complementary reconnaissance on sea and land.

8. There can be no question of peacetime privileges for any headquarters or formation of the armed services in coastal areas, or for any non-military organisations and units. The accommodation, security precautions, equipment, immediate readiness for action, and the

use they make of the ground in their area will entirely depend upon the need to meet any enemy attack as quickly and in as great strength as possible. Where the military situation demands it, the civilian population will be immediately evacuated.

III Competence of Commanders

1. The following are responsible for the preparation and execution of plans for coastal defence in the areas under German command:

(a) In the eastern area of operations (excluding Finland): the army commanders appointed by the OKH.

(b) In the coastal area of the AOK Lappland: C-in-C AOK, Lappland.

(c) In Norway: Commander Wehrmacht, Norway.

(d) In Denmark: Commander of German troops in Denmark.

(e) In the occupied western territories (incl the Netherlands): C-in-C West.

(For coastal defence the responsible commanders in (d) and (e) will be directly subordinate to the OKW.)

(f) In the Balkans (including the occupied islands): Commander Armed Forces Southeast.

(g) In the Baltic Territories and the Ukraine: Commander Armed Forces Baltic Territories and Ukraine.

(h) In the home theatre of war: the commanding admirals.

2. The commanders named in paragraph III-1 above will have for these tasks full powers of command over staffs commanding all armed forces, the German civil authorities and the non-military units and organisations in the area. In exercising this authority they will send out the necessars tactical, administrative and supply instructions, and ensure that they are obeyed. In all matters relating to land fighting, training of units will follow their dictates and all necessary information will be put at their disposal.

3. Among the orders to be given and measures to be taken the following must be given top priority:

(a) The inclusion inside fortified areas of strongpoints of all important military and industrial establishments that are concerned with defence, especially those of the Kriegsmarine (eg submarine bases) and Luftwaffe.

(b) The co-ordination of coastal reconnaissance.

(c) The defence of fortified areas and strongpoints by infantry.

(d) The defence by infantry of all isolated positions outside the fortified areas and strongpoints, eg coastal lookout posts and air-attack warning posts.

(e) Artillery defence against land targets. NB: The Kriegsmarine has priority in the installation of new batteries or conversion of existing batteries.

(f) The defensive preparedness, development and supply facilities of installations, including isolated posititons away from these installations. (This includes being equipped with all the necessary weapons needed for defence such as mines, hand grenades, flamethrowers barbed-wire, etc.)

(g) The signals communications network.

(h) Methods of ensuring that troops are alwavs on the alert and that infantry and gunnery training is being carried out in accordance with the special defence requirements.

4. Similar authority is conferred upon local commanders, up to sector commanders, in so far as they are responsible for the defence of a part of the coast. The commanders designated in paragraph III-1 will, in general, appoint commanders of army divisions employed in coastal defence as local commanders with full powers. In Crete, the Fortress Commandant Crete will appoint them. As far as other duties allow, local commandants or Luftwaffe/Kriegsmarine commanders will be made responsible for the general defence of individual sectors or sub-sectors, especially air and naval strongpoints.

5. All naval and air units employed in strategic warfare are subordinate to the Kriegsmarine or Luftwaffe. In the event of enemy attacks on the coast they are required to comply with the orders of the commanders responsible for defence, in so far as tactical considerations permit. They must therefore, be included in the distribution of all the information they for the duties, and close liaison will be maintained with their headquarters.

IV. Special Duties of the branches of the Wehrmacht in the field of Coastal Defence

1. Kriegsmarine

(a) Organisation and protection of coastal traffic.

(b) Training and employment of all coastal artillery against targets at sea.

(c) Employment of naval forces.

2. Luftwaffe

(a) Air defence of coastal areas. The use against enemy landings of suitable and available anti-aircraft guns, under the orders of the commander responsible for local defence, will not be affected.

(b) The completion of ground organisations and their protection against air attack and surprise attack by land; the latter in cases where airfields are not included in coastal defences and are therefore insufficiently protected.

(c) Operational employment of aircraft. Attention to be paid to duplication of connnand implied by these special duties.

V. Orders and instructions which run contrary to this directive are hereby cancelled with effect from 1 April 1942.

New operational orders which will be issued by commanders on the basis of my directive, are to be submitted to me through the OKW.

Signed: Adolf Hitler

end of 1941 after falling out with Hitler only to be recalled in July 1942 to become C-in-C West, was really only in command on paper; every major decision was actually made by Hitler or 'rubber-stamped' on his behalf. It is said that von Rundstedt once caustically remarked that the only troop formation he was actually allowed to move was the guard at the gate of his own headquarters.

Just a few days after the issue of Directive 40 the Kriegsmarine issued an order:

'Even if the fight for the coast extends to the coastal areas within reach of the Heer medium-range artillery, control over the bombardment of targets at sea remains in the hands of naval shore commanders who have command over coastal artillery (including Heer coastal artillery) in the sector for this purpose. The naval shore commanders are under the operational command of the respective Heer divisional commanders only in the battle for the coast.'

This muddled thinking produced a duality of command that might have worked in a straightfoward situation such as the one that pertained on the Channel Islands, where there was a clear demarcation between sea and land targets, the Kriegsmarine being responsible for engaging the enemy when they were on the water whilst the Heer took over once they had landed. Anti-aircraft guns were obviously excluded and could engage enemy aircraft with impunity. Thus the Kriegsmarine C-in-C Channel Islands (SEEKO–KI) exercised command over all Kriegsmarine and Heer coastal artillery, controlling their fire as and when necessary. However, this system of command for the defence of the Channel Islands against a determined enemy attack was never fully put to the test, although it does seem to have worked well enough within the tight limits of the small attacks on these tiny islands.

On the French coast, however, it was a different matter. Here the Heer wished to group its coastal batteries inland some 3 miles (5km) from the coast in order to reduce the risk from naval bombardment, whereas the naval commanders wanted their batteries to be situated as close to the coast as possible in order to be able to fire with line of sight directly upon assaulting enemy vessels. The resulting differences of opinion undoubtedly affected results. For example, if one looks in detail at the results achieved by the formidable coastal artillery battery at Longues-sur-Mer (4 x 15.2cm naval guns), when faced by the Allied armada on D-Day, we can see that it failed to sink or even to damage a single vessel of the enemy amphibious strike force.

Above: *Generalfeldmarschall Gerd von Rundstedt was possibly the Third Reich's most significant general, leading forces in the invasions of Poland, France and Russia; commanding in the west from 1942 to July 1944 and then again September 1944 to March 1945; even the Battle of the Bulge was known as the Rundstedt offensive.*

Below: *Hitler fancied himself a great general, and his successes in 1939 and 1940 did little to dissuade him of this. Here, L–R, Keitel, Hitler, Jodl, and von Brauchitsch confer.*

Further Directives and Orders from the Führer

While Directive 40 was clearly the most important of Hitler's pronouncements as far as the Atlantic Wall was concerned, it was not the only one that affected the wall. There are a number of others which were issued subsequently and which had a definite bearing on all or part of the Wall and so need to be looked at here.

Directive 51 (3 November 1943)

By 1943, German forces were swallowed up in the vastness of Russia; events in the Middle East had also turned against them.

Now there was also the inevitability of having to fight on another front as the Americans and British built up for an attack across the Channel. Directive 51, therefore, opened with some sombre words:

'The hard and costly struggle against Bolshevism during the last two and a half years, which has involved the bulk of our military strength in the east, has demanded extreme exertions. The greatness of the danger and the general situation demanded it. But the situation has since changed. The danger in the east remains, but a greater danger now appears in the west: an Anglo-Saxon landing! In the east, the vast extent of the territory makes it possible for us to lose ground even on a large scale, without a fatal blow being dealt to the nervous system of Germany.

'It is very different in the west! Should the enemy succeed in breaching our defences on a wide front here, the immediate consequences would be unpredictable. Everything indicates that the enemy will launch an offensive against the Western Front of Europe, at the latest in spring, perhaps even earlier.'

Above: *The battery at Longues-sur-Mer was nearing completion on D-Day—the fire control bunker was unfinished and the telephone lines had been destroyed by Allied bombing. Armed with four 152mm naval guns, it had been built by the Kriegsmarine but was under Heer control when it was put out of action by Allied naval gunfire before being captured by British troops. Of the various coastal batteries one commentator said, 'The Atlantic Wall was armed with guns anything up to 50 years old from ten different nations with 28 different calibres ranging from 406 to 75mm. Any standardisation was therefore impossible.'*

Right: *Flak position on the Channel Islands.*

No longer could the western defences be weakened in favour of the other theatres. Hitler had decided to reinforce them, in particular the areas from where the 'long-range bombardment of England will begin'—the secret V-weapon sites—because he considered that it was there the decisive battle against the enemy landing forces would be fought. Diversionary attacks were noted as being possible on other fronts and he cited Denmark as being a possible location for a large-scale attack. Such an assault would initially require the whole of the enemy offensive strength being thrown against the German forces holding the coastline. Therefore, 'Only by intensive construction, which means straining available manpower and materials at home and in that occupied territories to the limit, can we strengthen our coastal defences in the short time which probably remains.'

The directive went on to delineate the ground weapons that would shortly be sent to Denmark and the other occupied areas in the west, such as heavy anti-tank guns, static armoured fighting vehicles (to be sunk into existing emplacements), coastal artillery, mines and other supplies. They would be concentrated at strongpoints in the most threatened areas on the coast, which meant that everyone had to accept that the defences in less threatened areas would not be improved. If and when the enemy attacked, then immediate heavy counter-attacks would be launched, so as to prevent them exploiting their landings and throw them back into the sea. Such emotive phrases as 'high fighting quality', 'attacking power' and 'mobility' were used to describe these counter-attack forces, whilst 'careful and detailed emergency plans' had to be drawn up. The Luftwaffe and Kriegsmarine must also play their part, 'with all forces at their disposal, regardless of losses'.

The directive then went into considerable detail as to what action the Führer expected the Heer, Luftwaffe, Kriegsmarine and SS to take, requiring them to submit their plans to him immediately for the follow-up action to be taken within the next three months. The Chief of the General Staff, the Inspector General of the Wehrmacht and the C-in-C West were specifically named for action under the Heer section. The plan for the distribution of weapons, tanks, SP guns, motor vehicles and ammunition on the Western Front and in Denmark was to be based on the following dictates:

Fortification Order for the Channel Islands

Issued by the Führer's office on 20 October 1941, it read as follows:

1. Operations on a large scale against the territories we occupy in the west are, as before, unlikely. Under pressure of the situation in the east, however, or for reasons of politics or propaganda, small-scale operations at any moment may be anticipated, particularly an attempt to regain possession of the Channel Islands, which are important to us for the protection of sea communications.

2. Counter-measures in the islands must ensure that any English attack fails before a landing is achieved, whether it is attempted by sea, by air or both together. The possibility of advantage being taken of bad visibility to effect a surprise landing must be borne in mind. Emergency measures for strengthening the defences have already been ordered and all branches of the forces stationed in the islands, except the Luftwaffe, are placed under the orders of the Commandant of the islands.

3. With regard to the permanent fortification of the islands, to convert them into an impregnable fortress (which must be pressed forward with the utmost speed) I give the following orders:

(a) The OKH is responsible for the fortifications as a whole and will, in the overall programme, incorporate construction for the Luftwaffe and the Kriegsmarine. The strength of the fortifications and the order in which they are erected will be based on the principles and the practical knowledge gained from building the Western Wall.

(b) For the Heer: it is important to provide a close network of emplacements, well concealed, and given flanking fields of fire. The emplacements must be sufficient for guns of a size capable of piercing armour plate 100mm thick, to defend against tanks which may attempt to land. There must be ample accommodation for stores and ammunition, for mobile diversion parties and for armoured cars.

(c) For the Kriegsmarine: one heavy battery on the islands and two on the French coast to safeguard the sea approaches.

(d) For the Luftwaffe: strongpoints must be created with searchlights and sufficient space to accommodate such AA units as are needed to protect all-important constructions.

(e) Foreign labour, especially Russians and Spaniards but also Frenchmen, may be used for the building works.

4. Another order will follow for the deportation to the continent of all Englishmen who are not natives of the islands, i.e. not born there.

5. Progress reports to be sent to me on the first day of each month, to the C-in-C of the Heer and directed to the Supreme Command of the OKW— Staff of the Führer, Division I.

Signed: Adolf Hitler

• All panzer and panzergrenadier divisions were to be assured of adequate mobility and equipped with 93 PzKpfwIV tanks or SP guns, plus strong anti-tank weapons, by the end of December 1943.

• 20th Luftwaffe Field Division was to be converted into an effective mobile offensive formation by the allocation of SP artillery also by the end of 1943.

• Waffen-SS Panzergrenadier Division Hitlerjugend, 21st Panzer Division, and the infantry and reserve divisions in Jutland were to be speedily brought up to strength.

• A further reinforcement of PzKpfwIV SP guns and heavy anti-tank guns would be made to panzer divisions in reserve divisions in the west and Denmark; this was also to include the SP artillery training unit in Denmark.

The Panzerfaust came in 30m, 60m (as here), 100m and 150m versions. A one-shot anti-tank weapon with a shaped-charge warhead that required little training to use, it proved very effective on its entry into service in 1943.

• An additional monthly allocation of 100 heavy anti-tank guns (7.5cm PaK 40 L/46 and 8.8cm PaK 43 L/71) of which half were to be SP, was to be made during November and December to the newly raised formations in the west.

• An increased weapons' allocation (to include approximately 1,000 machine guns) was to be made to ground forces engaged in coastal defence in the west and Denmark (to be co-ordinated with the withdrawal of equipment from units in sectors not under attack threat).

• A liberal supply of short-range anti-tank weapons (*Panzerfaust* and *Panzerschreck*) was to be made to formations in threatened areas.

• The firepower in artillery and anti-tank guns of units stationed in Denmark and along the coasts of occupied territories in the west was to be increased, whilst Heer artillery was to be strengthened.

• No units or formations stationed in the west and Denmark, nor any of the newly raised SP armoured artillery or anti-tank units in the west, were to be moved to other fronts without the Führer's approval.

Heer required actions

OB West Von Rundstedt was to carry out a series of exercises in the field to ensure that additional formations could be moved up from sectors that were not under attack and made capable of offensive action. Hitler stated that labour units employed on construction were to open and keep open the lines of communication (roads and railways) which had been destroyed by the enemy, making full use of the local population.

This order also applied to the Commander of German troops in Denmark, while the Chief of Army Equipment and the Commander of the Replacement Army were to raise regiment-sized battle groups in the home defence area from the men in training depots, or at Heer schools and so on, which were to be at 48 hours notice of being called up. All further personnel must be immediately ready to replace the heavy casualties that would be expected.

Luftwaffe required actions

The offensive and defensive power of the formations stationed in the west and Denmark was to be increased. This would be done by taking forces from flying units and AA units engaged in home defence, also from schools and training establishments. Ground establishments in southern Norway, Denmark, northwest Germany and the west were to be organised and supplied so that they were as decentralised as possible, to ensure that units were not exposed to enemy bombing at the start of major operations. This was especially important as far as fighter aircraft were concerned, which needed an increased number of emergency airfields. 'Particular attention will be paid to good camouflage.'

Kriegsmarine required actions

The Kriegsmarine was to draw up plans to bring into action all naval forces capable of attacking the enemy landing fleet. 'Coastal defences under construction will be completed with all possible speed and the establishment of additional coastal batteries and the laying of further obstacles on the flanks will be considered.'

As with the Luftwaffe the employment of everyone from schools, training establishments and other land establishments on security duties was emphasised. Special attention was to be paid to defence against enemy landings in Norway or Denmark, in particular to plans for using large numbers of submarines in northern sea areas, even if this caused a temporary diminution of these forces in the Atlantic.

SS required actions

The Reichsführer-SS was to test the preparedness of units of the Waffen-SS and the police and make preparations to raise battle-trained formations from those on training in reserve or recuperating in the home defence area.

Hitler closed Directive 51 with orders to the various senior officers he had named in the directive to report by 15 November on what steps they had taken and those they proposed to take.

Führer Order 11

This was a general order issued for guidance to Commandants of Fortified Area and Battle Commandants. There were a number of these already but on 9 January 1944 he designated a number of coastal areas from the Netherlands to the Gironde estuary in southwest France as 'Fortresses' and issued special instructions for their defence. They were:

The Netherlands: Den Helder, Ijmuiden, Hoek of Holland and Vlissingen (Flushing) on Walcheren, located at the entrance to the River Scheldt.

France: Dunkirk (Dunkerque), Calais, Boulogne, Le Havre, Cherbourg and St Mâlo along the Channel coast; the harbours of Brest, Lorient, St Nazaire, La Rochelle (with U-boat pens at nearby La Pallice) and Royan at the mouth of the Gironde along the Atlantic coastline. Then on 3 March, the Channel Islands were also given fortress status.

The gist of Hitler's Order 11 was as follows:
1. A distinction was to be made between *Festen Plätze* (Fortified Areas or Fortresses) which would be under a Fortified Area Commandant and *Ortsstützpunkte* (Local Strongpoints) each commanded by a Battle

On Grande Côte beach at St Palais-sur-Mer, Royan, Gi12 HKB Hamburg was armed with four 10.5cm K331(f) guns in open emplacements which are slowly subsiding towards the sea. Thierry Llansades

Commandant. The fortified areas were likened to castles of past eras, their aim being to ensure that the enemy did not occupy an area of vital operational importance. They would allow themselves to be surrounded and by doing so tie down the maximum possible number of enemy who would thus be liable to successful counter-attacks. Local strongpoints on the other hand were within the battle area and would be defended tenaciously in the event of enemy penetration. They would act as a reserve for defence and should the enemy breakthrough, as a corner/hinge for the front, becoming places from which counter-attacks could be launched.

2. Each Fortified Area Commandant was to be specially selected, a tough experienced soldier, preferably of the rank of general, and could not delegate his responsibilities. He would be appointed by, and personally responsible to, the Armeegruppe C-in-C. They would 'pledge their honour as soldiers to carry out their duties to the last'. The Armeegruppe C-in-C was the only person permitted to relieve a Fortified Area Commandant of his duties or to order him to surrender; however, this could not be done without Hitler's personal approval. Everyone within a Fortified Area was under the orders of the commandant, irrespective of their rank be they soldiers or civilians. The Fortified Area Commander had the military rights and disciplinary powers of a commanding general, with both mobile courts martial and civilian courts to assist him. His staff would be appointed by Armeegruppe while his chief of staff would be appointed by OKH, but in accordance with suggestions from the Armeegruppe.

3. The garrison of a fortified area comprised two elements: the security garrison and the general garrison. The former was to be inside the fortified area at all times. Its strength would depend on the size of the area and the tasks to be fulfilled (for example, preparation and completion of defences, holding the area against raids or local enemy attack). The strength would, like the security garrison, be laid down by the C-in-C Army Group, depending upon the size and task(s) of the fortified area.

4. Each Battle Commandant came under the orders of the local forces commander and would be appointed by him and was to receive his operational orders from him. His rank would depend on the importance of the position and the garrison strength. His duties called for 'specially energetic officers whose qualities have been proved in crisis.'

5. The strength of the garrison of a 'Local Strongpoint' was to be fixed by the importance of the positions and the available troops. Orders were to be given from the HQ to which the Battle Commandant was subordinate.

Hitler would go on to name more fortresses on the Eastern Front in March 1944.

Directive 62

This was the order for the strengthening of the German Bight defences and covered the following main points:

1. The area covered was the German coast from the Danish frontier to the Dutch frontier, as well as those of the North and East Frisian Islands which had not yet been fully fortified, while those that had been fortified were to be brought up to a full state of defence.

Defences of Le Havre showing barbed wire, anti-tank tetrahedra, and anti-tank wall. Along with minefields these were part of the defences in depth that Hitler expected all areas to construct.

2. The planning and preparation of all necessary measures for the speedy construction of a second position to run from the Danish frontier at a depth of about 10km from the coast.

3. The person responsible for construction was named as Gauleiter Kaufmann of Hamburg. However, this was later changed to make the Gauleiters of Schleswig-Holstein, East Hannover and Weser-Ems responsible for the defences which were located in their areas, whilst Kaufmann would supply them with what resources he had available and also act as their spokesman to X Corps.

4. C-in-C Naval Command North was to assume the direction of purely military tasks, with the Deputy General of X Army Corps responsible for carrying out the following tasks:

    (a) Planning the defensive system and estimating the materials needed for the construction of permanent field fortifications; also for estimating the strength of the garrison needed for a full defence.

    (b) Settling the tactical siting of the defence line in detail.

    (c) Establishing building priorities for the completion of the various sectors.

    (d) Deciding on the form which the construction would take in the light of past experience (technical and tactical) and what material was available.

5. In addition, Deputy General X Corps was to form three more planning staffs composed of officers of all arms, plus Engineer staffs including the Naval Fortification Engineer Organisation stationed in the German Bight.

6. As far as priorities for construction were concerned the following had top priority:

    (a) North and East Frisian Islands.

    (b) The coastal sector opposite Sylt (Hindenburgdamm).

    (c) The Eiderstedt peninsula.

    (d) The river defence of the Elbe-Weser estuary.

    (e) The coast Brunsbüttel-Cuxhaven-Wesermünde-Wilhelmshaven inclusive.

    (f) The Ems estuary with Delfzijl.

7. The remainder of the coastline had second priority.

8. The construction was to comprise a continuous anti-tank obstacle, with an articulated defensive system in depth that was to be continuously strengthened.

9. The Gauleiter was responsible for procuring and employing civilian labour, accommodating and feeding them (including OT).

10. The OT was to be employed on the basis of direct agreement between the Gauleiter and the OT. Local OT staff would be attached to Kaufmann's staff.

11. Gauleiter Kaufmann was to report to Hitler, via the Head of the Reich Chancellery, as soon as possible on his plans for organising the work and raising the labour. Naval High Command North Sea was to report on the 1st and 15th of each month (via OKW) on the state and progress of the construction.

The German S-boot (Schnellboot), termed E-boat by the Allies, proved an extremely useful warship for use in inshore operations with a number of Allied merchant ships, destroyers and other naval vessels sunk by mine-dropping or direct action. This is a photo of S 204 surrendering on 13 May 1945. S 204 had on board Korvettenkapitän Kurt Fimmen (CO of 4th Schnellboot-Flotilla).

1 BUILDING THE WALL

Above: *Konstantin Hierl was the commander of the RAD from the start. Two years before the Nazi party reached power, Hierl had taken charge of the* Freiwilliger Arbeitsdienst *(FAD), a state-sponsored labour organization of which there were many in Europe during the Great Depression.*

Below: *Cover of the OT newspaper,* Der Frontarbeiter, *dated 24 July 1943.* J.P. Benamou Collection

The Wall Builders: Organisations

Organisation Todt was mainly responsible for much of building work, but it was actually only one of a number elements concerned with the overall building programme. These were:

Reichsarbeitsdienst (RAD—State Labour Service)
The RAD was sometimes involved in fortification work. In speeches before he came to power, Hitler had promised that he would overcome unemployment (*Arbeitslosigkeit*), and did so simply by making labour on behalf of the state compulsory. A law was passed on 16 June 1935 which made it obligatory for all non-Jewish German men between the ages of 18 and 25 to work in the *RAD/Männer* for six months before their two years military service (conscription had been reintroduced on 21 May 1935). RAD/M also contained some volunteers as well as the mass of conscripts; these volunteers stayed for at least a year. All were under the command of a cadre of Army officers and NCOs who had already completed their military service. The first annual contingents numbered 200,000 men. There was also the *RAD der weiblichen Jugend* (RAD/wJ) for young women.

Many men were assigned to farms to work under a strict regime with no distinction being made between workers, artisans, peasants or intellectuals. Women who were called up did housework in peasant homes while the men worked in the fields. In this way, Hitler reduced Germany's unemployment from six million to one million in just over a year, producing at the same time a pool of cheap labour as all were paid just a nominal wage. He saw it also as a necessary step towards rearmament—'men who shouldered shovels would one day carry guns'.

In 1938, the RAD/M was organised in Divisional Districts (*Arbeitsgaue*) I–XXXII, each commanded by a brigadier, with a staff and an HQ guard company and some eight battalions of 1,200–1,800 men, each under a lieutenant-colonel or a major. The normal work unit was company-sized, containing 200 men with an HQ and four platoons, each with 17-man sections under a sergeant/corporal, although the ranks in the RAD were actually different from those of the Wehrmacht. The men all carried spades and their transport was normally by bicycle. Pre-World War 2, the RAD supported armed forces in the invasions of Austria, the Sudetenland and Czechoslovakia. From June 1938 to September 1939, 300 companies also worked in conjunction with civilian contractors under the OT building the Siegfried Line (*Westwall*) along western border from Emmerich (frontier with the Netherlands) to Lörrach (ditto with Switzerland). About a hundred companies assisted with similar work on the Ostwall fortifications on the Polish border.

In August 1939, when general mobilisation was declared, the RAD was at its peak strength, with 360,000 men in 1,700 companies. Almost straight away well over 60% (1,050 companies) were transferred to the Heer to form *Bautruppen*. Following on from the end of the Polish campaign, Hitler ordered the RAD to be rebuilt, which meant that the RAD went back to its prewar status of providing pre-military training and, at the same time, supporting Heer engineers.

By 1940 there were 39 *Arbeitsgaue,* Numbers XXXIII–XXXIX being in Austria and Bohemia. Later the RAD was active in all theatres, some companies being sent to France to help build the Atlantic Wall and further into in the war they even manned AA batteries, laid minefields and manned and defended fortifications, as well as building defensive earthworks along the German borders from August to October 1944. This action caused the Allies to protest that the RAD was abusing non-combatant status under the Geneva Convention.

'Men who shouldered shovels would one day carry guns.' The RAD in 1940. Rolf Munninger of Fellbach joined Abteilung 306-3 in Rohrbach/Holledu in Bavaria. He remembers that they had 'plenty of sport and training, but also plenty of work too!' For example, they straightened and regulated the River Ilm, dug a trench in which Siemens technicians were to lay a cable from Donaueschingen to Freiburg, built a dam where there had been a bridge between Breisach and Colmar, and repaired bomb-damaged flats in villages in Alsace. Then, at the end of his RAD service, he was called up for the Heer. Without doubt RAD service made the transition from civilian to service life much easier as the men had become used to hard work, discipline and obeying orders.

Divisional Field Engineers (Pioniere)

While ordinary individual members of Heer units, especially infantrymen, were responsible for constructing field fortifications such as weapon pits, foxholes and trenches, the Heer's badged engineers, the *Pioniere,* were responsible for a wide range of duties such as bridging, ferrying, demolitions, the construction of obstacles and, as far as their responsibilities within the building programme were concerned, all aspects of the distribution, recording and sowing of land mines, plus the location and use of flame-throwers.

Army Construction Battalions (Baubataillone)

Responsible for reinforced field-type constructions which were designed to withstand and to give protection from bullets, shell-splinters and blast, but not prolonged attack.

Fortress Engineers and Fortress Construction Battalions (Festungsbautruppen)

Responsible for supplying and mounting fortress weapons, the *Festungsbautruppen* also conveyed heavy loads, tunnelled, compiled construction progress reports and maps, and ordered and supervised tasks undertaken by the OT. In overall command of them was the *Festungspionierkommandeur General der Pioniere der Festungen und der Eisenbahnpioniere* (Fortress Engineer Commander General of Fortress Engineers and Railway Engineers) Alfred Jacob. He held this post for the whole war and his units contained experts in all branches of military engineering. In every defence district (*Wehrkreis*) in Germany there were Fortress Engineer units, Fortress Construction Battalions, and Construction Battalions. Their units contained experts in all branches of military engineering such as tunnelling, camouflage, reinforced concrete work, geology, artillery.

Organisation Todt (OT)

The OT was responsible for quarrying, most tunnelling projects, constructing power stations, railways and roads, supplying building, equipment and machinery, organising sea transport (in conjunction the Kriegsmarine), loading and unloading ships, supervising civilian construction firms, controlling non-military labour and building fortress-type constructions. *Ministerialdirektor* (a civil service grade equivalent to the rank of

Franz Xaver Dorsch was born in Bavaria on 24 December 1899. In 1934 he was appointed District Advisor to the OT in Berlin. In 1939 he was placed in charge of all construction work on the western frontiers of Germany. Two years later he became Deputy Chief of the OT and in 1944 Chief of the OT Construction Office. In May 1945 he was taken prisoner by US forces at Tegernsee, Bavaria.

lieutenant-general) Franz Dorsch became deputy chief of the OT in 1941. Captured by the Americans at the end of the war, whilst in prison Dorsch volunteered to write about the OT for the Foreign Military Studies Branch of the US Army Historical Division European Command. This resulted in Document MS P-037, in which he discussed the foundation of the OT:

'When Hitler ordered the construction of the Westwall to be accelerated in the spring of 1938, the fortress engineer staffs in charge of this work were, because of the magnitude of the project and their lack of experience in large-scale construction, quite understandably and excusably at first unable to cope with the business side of the job: the control and allocation of contractors and workmen, the distribution and transportation of materials and the other minor tasks connected with these things. Therefore, he appointed Dr. Todt, then Inspector General of the German Highway System, to carry out this task. The reasons for the selection of Dr. Todt are obvious.

'Besides his mastery of the principles of construction engineering, Dr. Todt, as Inspector General of the German Highway System, was the man who had laid the organisational foundation which enabled the German construction, building materials and construction machinery industry; after years of very low output—one might even say after years of economic decline—to rise to exceptional achievements in a short time in connection with the construction of the national autobahn system, with the result that after 1936 about 1,000km of autobahn were completed every year. This achievement was primarily due to the fact that Todt, who himself was a man from private industry, opened the way to free enterprise from bureaucratic restrictions and encouraged it in every way. Furthermore, in spite of his individual treatment of autobahn engineering, for example with respect to adapting the construction to the landscape and other aesthetic considerations, he succeeded to a far-reaching degree by standardising construction works and construction equipment depots, which, judging by conditions in Germany, certainly had to be regarded as a great step forward in the field of construction engineering.

'An additional important point was that since the national autobahns covered great distances and were frequently far from any residential areas of any size, it was necessary to quarter large numbers of workmen quickly and efficiently in new, temporary camps. Under the direction of Dr. Todt work was done in this field which was a model of its kind. Recognition of this work of Dr. Todt's was given expression in the so-called "Law Governing the Accommodating of Workmen in Construction Projects." The general standards for the accommodation of autobahn workmen were thereby declared binding in connection with construction projects in general.'

Dorsch goes on to describe Todt's work in connection with the building of the Westwall, where construction works totalling around 8 million cubic metres of concrete and reinforced concrete had to be completed within a relatively short time. Just as with constructing major highways, two of the main tasks were rapid labour procurement and workers' accommodation. It would hardly have been possible to find a more suitable man than Todt to solve the economic and logistic problems concerned with the construction of the Westwall.

From Dorsch's report one can summarise the expansion of the OT thus: its origins begin in the autobahn-building organisation gathered together by Fritz Todt in 1933, which was honed, improved and expanded by Todt over the next five years, when, still without a name, it was sent to assist the Army Fortress Engineers in constructing the Westwall along Germany's border with France. In June 1938 Todt began to recruit a whole raft of civilian firms into his organisation and organised them into brigades— known as *Oberbauleitungen* (Senior Construction Administrations). Then, on 18 July 1938, Hitler first called the body the Organisation Todt (OT), although the men still did not wear uniforms. For a while the OT remained behind the Westwall repairing railways, roads and bridges, and gaining its status as an auxiliary to the armed forces. Then, as the German forces spread throughout Europe, the OT followed with its 200,000 men, (still mainly German). However, as it grew larger, the German element became the planners and overseers now wearing khaki uniforms and special badges, whilst the majority of the labourers were either foreign volunteers or forced labourers. This distinction became more pronounced when Hitler issued an order to say that in future the menial tasks—such as breaking up stones or carrying bags of cement—were no longer to be done by Germans.

By 1943, the OT was over a million strong and growing fast. The change from Todt to Speer made little difference to the smooth running of the OT, although Speer did put it onto a more regular footing, so that it now had its own weapons (for self-protection, especially in areas where partisans were very active) and its own medical services. The grievous casualties suffered by the armed forces did cause a major change in that more and more German members—officials and overseers—were called up for military service. Their places were taken by foreign volunteers and, in some cases, by ex-penal-unit personnel. The foreigners who joined often did so in order to escape being deported to Germany or (if Jewish) being sent to die in a concentration camp. This led to a wide range of different nations being represented in the OT, alongside ethnic Germans. These included Allied prisoners of war; people from the European countries nearest to Germany—such as the Netherlands, Denmark, Belgium and Norway; and those from further away such as from Italy and the Balkans, Russia and the Ukraine. The largest foreign group were ex-Soviet citizens. Thomas and Jurado's book *Wehrmacht Auxiliary Forces* lists the breakdown of the OT in November 1944, when it had reached its maximum as being:

German	44,000	+313,000 in contracted firms	357,000
Foreign	12,800	+680,700 in contracted firms	693,500
Women (German)	4,000		4,000
POW	165,000		165,000
Petty criminals	140,000	(a category which included Jews)	140,000
Totals	365,800	+993,700	1,359,500

As far as the Atlantic Wall was concerned, there were OT workers employed in all areas, stretching from Einsatzgruppe Wiking with units in Norway and Denmark, right along to France where there were some 112,000 German and 152,000 French workers, including 17,000 from the French North African colonies.

OT Work in Northwest Europe
Dorsch lists the work done by the OT from the French Armistice onwards as being:

Canals and Seaports
General repairs to the network of canals, particularly in the region of northern France and Belgium. Within the scope of this work OT also undertook the clearing and repair of various seaports, such as Boulogne, Calais and Dunkirk. Tackled in parallel was the construction of shatterproof oil reservoirs in the various ports in the Bay of Biscay, and construction of bombproof shelters for the more important harbour personnel and quarters for the troops. The OT also took over the construction of airfields in the zone of Regional Air Command for Brussels.

Emplacing the heavy batteries on Cap Gris-Nez
We have already covered these 'Sealion' guns. However, from an OT point of view it began with the emplacement of some 20 heavy calibre guns

Born at Pforzheim, Baden, into an upper class family, in World War 1 Dr. Todt served in the Deutsche Luftstreit-kräfte, (German Army Air Force). Postwar he ended up in a Munich firm which specialised in building roads and tunnels. A member of the Nazi Party from 1922, soon after Hitler came to power Todt was put in charge of the new state-owned Reichs-autobahnen corporation and ordered to build a national highway system—laid out by the military and primarily for military use, but of course with enormous beneficial use for civilians. Todt helped to found the Nationalsozialistischer Bund Deutscher Technik and co-ordinated all the engineers and managers of the German construction industry into a single, enormous entity—Organisation Todt. From late 1941, he was also given responsibity for restoring the railways and road system in occupied Russia. In his capacity as head of OT he was, until his death in 1942, in charge of the major construction works on the Atlantic Wall. He died on 8 February 1942 in an aircraft accident and his position was taken on by Speer.

Hitler's favourite architect was the son and grandson of successful architects. Albert Speer was some years younger than Todt and was an instant hit with the Führer who became a firm admirer of the tall architect and gave him such commissions as designing the Reichstag building and the Nuremberg stadium in which the most spectacular Nazi ceremonies were performed. In his memoirs he commented that if Hitler had had any friends he would certainly have been considered one of his closest. The shy, retiring Speer hated making speeches and had no interest in fame. However, he did covet power and lost no time in taking over the reins when Todt was killed—and he had to move fast because power-hungry competitors like Goering were waiting in the wings to step in. Speer was responsible for continued miracles and lasted out the war. Speer is considered by some to be a 'good Nazi', especially as he 'owned up' to his share of what the Nazis had done. However, this did not stop him being found guilty of war crimes and crimes against humanity because he had knowingly used slave labour. Waiving his right to appeal, he spent 20 years in prison and was released in 1966. He died in 1981.

and the construction of subsidiary installations (quarters for personnel, medical facilities, ammunition bunkers and so on) in a semi-permanent manner (2m thick ferro-concrete). All this work had to be completed in eight weeks while the guns remained without cover, The next demand was that, without interfering with their readiness for action, the guns were to be provided with a 3.5m thick ferro-concrete roof and additional subsidiary installations. The first phase had required the handling of some 30,000cu m of ferro-concrete, but the second phase was much longer, dragged on until the spring of 1941 and involved some 130,000cu m of ferro-concrete, so a total of 160,000cu m was used at Cap Gris-Nez alone.

Constructing U-boat shelters

In autumn 1940 the OT received orders from Hitler to build bombproof U-boat shelters on the Atlantic coast, beginning at the ports of Brest, Lorient and St Nazaire. In 1943 these were extended to include shelters at Marseille and Toulon in the Mediterranean. In the main the Engineer and Fortification General drew up the patterns for the types of shelter, then these were forwarded to the OT for it to draft and work out the construction plans in detail. Some 96 bombproof berths were built, including requisite workshops, covered locks and other subsidiary installations. A further 33 were under construction when the invasion began.

Construction of the Atlantic Wall

In autumn 1941 the OT received orders to start construction work on the Channel Islands, as Hitler feared the enemy might regain possession of the islands which would then be a constant menace to the north coast of France and be able to provide an excellent 'jumping off place' for the enemy once the invasion began. Then in 1942, came the Directive 40, which was as Hitler put it: 'the clear-cut conception of the Atlantic Wall defence system'. He went on to explain that the development of the wall was based upon the following basic principles:

1. Under all circumstances interference with traffic in the U-boat bases was to be prevented, even if an invasion should initially be successful. Work on unfinished bases must continue and the bases equipped for all round defence.

2. Every port that could serve for large-scale landings must be rendered inaccessible to the enemy, so as to compel him to carry out all landing operations on the unprotected coast and hence under less favourable conditions than within a harbour. Therefore the all-round defence of all ports within the framework of the Atlantic Wall was essential.

3. Defensive power must be concentrated as far forward as possible, that is close to the coastline, so as to tackle the enemy at his weakest moment, namely whilst landing. It also meant being able to reach as far as possible seawards with artillery.

4. Wherever possible guns were to be provided with ferro-concrete roofs as protection against air attacks. The objection to this was that it would considerably restrict fields of fire and make all-round fire impossible, but Hitler discounted this with the remark that in the event of an air attack meeting with only limited success, the guns could be put out of action by just a few large fragments. (As we shall see later, in the Assessment chapter, this proved to be incorrect.)

5. The basic principle underlying the technical equipment, the choice of location and the type of installations was the same as in the case of the Westwall, namely that: 'The final struggle for the position is fought by the infantry', and therefore provision had to be made for adequate and secure shelter space for them, where they could weather out the shelling and bombing preceding any enemy close-combat attacks, without their combat efficiency being reduced.

Prior to Minister Speer talking with Hitler, Dorsch had given him an estimate of 450,000cu m/month of ferro-concrete as being the highest figure the OT could handle—after a few months getting things underway. Later Speer, to be on the safe side, reduced this figure to 300,000cu m/month on all projects including the U-boat pens. In fact, the amount of ferro-concrete work done by the OT between July 1940 and July 1944, was a staggering 25 million cubic metres. The OT did not carry out the work itself, but rather had all the work entrusted to be carried out by firms of building contractors. Even the manpower employed by the 'Mobile OT' was supplied by firms.

The OT was not directly under the command of the Wehrmacht, but was treated as a subsidiary organisation (*Wehrmachtsgefolge*) because, lacking the facilities granted in the war zone and the occupied territories, otherwise it would have encountered extreme difficulties. As a subsidiary organisation to the Wehrmacht, OT personnel could travel on Wehrmacht tickets and it could have its supplies shipped on Wehrmacht consignment notes. It also had the right to demand Wehrmacht billeting facilities, to use Wehrmacht telephone and cable lines and all other installations of the Wehrmacht. It was subject to the directives issued by the Wehrmacht command agencies in respect of its actions in the war zone and so forth. Direct subordination of the OT to any one of the branches of the Wehrmacht was not possible because the organisation had to work for all three branches of the Wehrmacht and also on a comparatively large scale for the Ministry of Armaments, a further reason why it needed its own facilities for its connections with the building industry and for procurement of supplies etc. Hence the OT accepted definite contracts from the Armed Forces and then had to fulfil them on its own responsibility.

As far as the Atlantic Wall was concerned, an agreement was reached at the end of 1942 concerning the construction work between the General of Engineers and Fortifications in OKH, Alfred Jacob, and HQ OT. According to this the sites were to be chosen solely by Fortress Engineer staffs, while the building contractors then to do the work were chosen by the OT Construction Group Chief. Dorsch wrote:

ERBAUT NACH WEISUNGEN
DES FÜHRERS
ADOLF HITLER
FÜR DEN BEFEHLSHABER
DER UNTERSEE-BOOTE
VIZEADMIRAL DÖNITZ
U· SEINE WAFFE DURCH
DIE ORGANISATION TODT
BAUBEGINN FEBRUAR 1941
⚡EINFAHRT DES ERSTEN⚡
U·BOOTES: I·AUGUST 1941
UBERGABE DER ANLAGE:
AM 20·DEZEMBER 1941 ⚡

Above and Below: *The submarine pens were not directly part of the Atlantic Wall, but their construction was ringfenced by Hitler as a top OT priority. From 1941 huge amounts of materiel and a significant proportion of the OT workforce was involved as pens were built in France at Bordeaux, Brest, Lorient (as* **Above***), Saint Nazaire, and La Rochelle; in Norway at Bergen and Trondheim; and in Germany on Helgoland and at Bremen, Danzig, Hamburg, Kiel and Wilhelmshaven. Construction of the 11-pen Bordeaux bunker (***Below***) began in autumn 1941 and was completed in summer 1943.*

This Arbeitsbuch Für Ausländer (Workbook for foreigner) identity document was issued to a forced labourer in 1942. The letter "P" patch identified that he was a Pole, and he was required to wear the patch to identify himself from the German population in the areas foreigners were forced to work in Germany. Sjam2004/ Wiki

'A decisive factor, in the Atlantic Wall construction was the approval given on 22 August 1942, by the Chief of Staff OB West, General Kurt Zeitzler, to construction work being continued until 1 May 1943 in such manner as though no landing by the enemy were expected by that date. This approval made the serial mass production of the construction parts possible on a purely building economical basis, without regard to the combat efficiency of the installations at any given moment, whereby an increased capacity was brought about. Thus, in April 1943, the record was reached—870,000cu m of ferro-concrete work being completed in that month.'

He goes on to explain that the reason for the decrease in output after that date was due to the necessity, starting in May 1943, to repair the Mohne and Eder Valley dams which had been destroyed by the RAF. A considerable part of the construction capacity was transferred from the wall to Construction Group 'Ruhr' (it took OT four and a half months to repair the dams). Dorsch also says that, in all, some 10,400,000cu m of ferro-concrete work were built into the Atlantic Wall.

In reply to criticisms that the Atlantic Wall was too thin or not deeply enough organised, Dorsch points out that from the constructional point of view it would hardly have been possible under the circumstances pertaining after 1942 to achieve any better capacities for ferro-concrete work except at the expense of other military or war industry structures. Had work begun immediately after the French armistice, then the picture would have entirely different. Dorsch says that towards the end of 1943, he had drawn Hitler's attention to the fact that it would be necessary to slow down work on the wall, because in an emergency it would be impossible to man it. Hitler asked him how many bunkers would be available in the completed wall and how many men they could accommodate on average. He had replied that at best there would be 15,000 bunkers with a capacity of six men in each, to which Hitler replied (to Keitel) that this figure would not even suffice to hold the staffs! Actually the OT handed over 9,671 'ready to occupy' bunkers (minimum 2m ferro-concrete), and 5,976 field-type bunkers, so the total was 15,647. In addition, the concrete work had been done on a further 1,386 permanent and 205 field bunkers before the invasion began.

Of course the OT was not left alone at any time to concentrate on the wall. Dorsch mentions the building of U-boat bases, E-boat bases, various structures for the Luftwaffe, plus such work as the bauxite mines in Brignoles, near Marseille, and tungsten mining at Fougères. He also mentions the launching sites and servicing installations for V-1 and V-2 missiles including dummy sites, and construction of the so-called Millipede (*Tausendfüßler*)—a long-range gun with 12 x 160m barrels. In addition to 'other work' the OT also had to put up with enemy interference: the V-weapon sites at St Omer, for example, being repeatedly attacked with heavy bombs and totally destroyed.

The Wall Builders: The Workers

Whilst German fortress engineers, both military and civilian, German industry and the OT provided the expert guidance for building the wall, the men who toiled and did the hard manual labour came from many different countries. They were certainly not all just 'thousands of Russian slave workers from the east' as popular folklore imagines, although there were quite enough Russians in the system to see how such a rumour came about. However, there were also many others from all over the world. In general terms, they can be divided into the categories of volunteers (including local volunteers), conscripts, slave workers, PoWs and locals.

Volunteers and Conscripts

OT set up recruiting offices all over 'Greater Germany' and was soon offering employment to suitable volunteers. The bait used was a combination of good pay, plus good rations at the 'heavy worker' rate, and even periods of home leave. Volunteers had to sign a contract to serve for 6, 9 or 12 months, and many thousands did so. In the main they were skilled tradesmen—for example blacksmiths, carpenters, clerks and draughtsmen—who were undoubtedly worthy of their hire. However, as Michael Ginns points out:

'Some were in the Resistance and joined so that they could have access to OT plans and pass on information to London; others were at the opposite end of the political scale, being supporters of Fascism who wanted Germany to win the war anyway.'

He goes on to explain that one of the biggest boosts to OT recruitment in occupied France was the *Service Travail Obligatoire* (STO—Compulsory Work Service) under which those called up for work in factories might find themselves having to work in Germany. They hoped that by volunteering for the OT they would stay in France, but this did not always happen. By November 1943, there were 1,144,000 French males and 44,000 French females working in German factories. Moreover, on 5 January 1944 Friedrich 'Fritz' Sauckel, who directed the mobilisation of German and foreign workers from 1942 onwards, said that he planned to draft a further million Frenchmen to work in Germany. Similar Saukel decrees had gone into operation in Holland on 6 April 1942 and in Belgium on 6 October.

For example, a group of four Dutchmen who had worked in the Channel Islands and France and then arrived in the UK from Normandy on 19 July 1944, were interviewed. One had been a bookkeeper, another a carpenter, a third a greengrocer and the fourth a labourer. They had been part of a large contingent of Dutchmen sent to France for OT labour. Some then went to the Channel Islands, stayed about a year, but were then returned to the mainland. They had been employed by the Dutch firm of Boslond & De Wolf although neither of the firm's partners ever came to the islands. All the Dutch firms were subcontractors for the German firm of Wolfer & Goebel. When in Alderney the men were stationed in Norderney Camp, which housed workers of all nationalities. By January 1943 there were some 900 men in this camp, including just over 150 Germans and a few Frenchmen. The rest were Russians until in September 1943 when 300 Jews arrived.

Arbitary beatings by the OT staff were a daily occurrence at the Nordeney Camp and in other camps on Alderney.

'The beatings were carried out with fist, foot, stick, piece of hosepipe or other weapon. The reasons given were for trivial breaches of the harsh regulations and often there was no palpable reason at all.'

Major Bunny Pantcheff quotes from two victims who survived in his book *Alderney, Fortress Island*:

'Every day the Camp Commandant made a habit of beating any man he found not standing properly to attention or who had not made his bed properly or who did not execute a drill movement properly. The beatings were carried out on the head, face or body with a stick about 2.5cm in diameter. The Camp Commandant's assistant also beat workers daily with a stick of the same thickness on all parts of the body until their faces were covered in blood and they could not rise from the ground, when he would call on the prisoner's mates to carry the prostrate body away... In October 1942, there was an occasion when a carrot was thrown from a window by one of the cooks and was picked up by a Russian who was beaten mercilessly with a stick and then kicked while lying on the ground.'

"Fritz" Sauckel was Gauleiter of Thuringia and the General Plenipotentiary for Labour Deployment from 1942 until 1945. He was one of the 24 Major War Criminals who went before the International Military Tribunal at Nuremberg. He blamed Speer, but was found guilty and hanged.

The treatment of the slave labour by the SS was undoubtedly worse than that meted out to any other workers; they were truly at the very bottom of the pile and suffered accordingly. To quote Major Pantcheff again:

'The significant feature of life in practice in the undernourished labour force was, as one inmate put it: "Within a month and a half of my arrival at Norderney Camp the average death rate was 2–3 per day. At the time of our arrival we had all been in normal health, but constant beatings and starvation diet had reduced us to an extremely feeble condition."'

The Netherlands and Belgium also provided volunteers for the OT and these were also encouraged to work in German factories, initially by an intense propaganda scheme, but then by the withholding of unemployment benefits from those unwilling to go. As Walter B. Maass says in his book *The Netherlands at War 1940–45*:

'Until 1942 no one was actually forced to relocate to Germany. Prices and wages were at first frozen, later moderate increases granted... Another new institution was a German type of labor service originally introduced to act as a sort of manpower pool for demobilized army personnel, with the task of repairing war damage. Later compulsory labor service for all Dutch boys at the age of 18 was decreed... It was this last piece of German legislation that affected the greatest number of people. At first, all underemployed persons under the age of 40 were compelled to register. Then German task forces started combing Dutch factories for men who would be useful in armament plants in the Reich. Workers who refused to relocate were placed in labor camps or simply transported to Germany. The labor draft became more and more an outright deportation, and the railroad stations were often filled with weeping women and children who saw their husbands, fathers and brothers depart for a very uncertain future... On May 25 (1942) a new regulation ordered all men between 18 and 35 to register for work in Germany. Three age groups were promptly called up and transported to Germany.'

Above: *Bunker numbering—three examples from AOK1: Inside a 622 of Gi302, Le Verdon sur Mer (***Top***); in S473–S483 Turm Dora—an emplacement for a 20.3cm gun, part of MKB Karola (***Centre***); and a 502 of Ro 425 HKB Kora, both on the Île de Ré (***Below***).* Thierry Llansades

Below: *Divisional Field Engineers had a wide range of duties including the construction of obstacles. Elsewhere Heer construction battalions were responsible for reinforced-type constructions. These soldiers are hard at work building defences in Normandy in 1943.* J.P. Benamou Collection

There was no escaping this decree, because Dutch employers were expressly forbidden to take on new staff without permission from the labour office.

Among the forced labourers were several thousand Spanish Nationalists who had fought in the Spanish Civil War against Franco. One of these was Juan Taule who had escaped over the frontier into France and was 'given' (his own word) to the Germans by the French authorities in late 1940 in exchange for the release of French POWs. He was initially employed working on the submarine base at La Rochelle, but after some six months was taken over to Jersey and billeted in Elizabeth Castle, St Helier. First of all, he worked on sea walls around the castle, then moved to various other locations, staying longest at Camp Udet, Route de Orange, where he worked on bunkers and sea walls at La Carriere Point, St Ouen's Bay, and other places. Working conditions were not good and food was scarce, especially in 1943–44. Fortunately the foreman who was with the gang all the time was, as Taule put it, 'one of the "good" Germans' and treated them reasonably well: 'We were lucky to get him.' Juan Taule actually worked for the German company Kehl & Co, who had set up a branch on the Channel Islands, in line with many other German building firms.

Slave Labourers

'Very little distinction seems to have been made by the Germans between Russian war prisoners and forced labour mobilised in the towns and in the villages from the civil population in occupied territory. They have all been treated with the same brutality, undernourished, a very large proportion worked to death and many beaten to death.'

That is how MI19 (RPS) report 2292 on 'Forced Labour—Prison Atrocities' dated 25 July 1944 begins. (MI19 was set up to interrogate POWs and at the end of the war reported on the German occupation of the Channel Islands.) It was compiled from the experiences of 14 Red Army soldiers and Russian civilians, all of whom without exception told of 'torture, starvation and very hard work.' However, they also said that the Germans had slack control over both POWs and forced labour, not only when they were still

Juan Taule (arrowed) with a group of Spanish forced labourers 'acquired' by the OT. He worked first on the submarine pens at La Rochelle before being shipped over to Jersey. J. Taule

in occupied Russian territory but also after they were taken to France and the Channel Islands.

'In Alderney, Jersey and Cherbourg, many prisoners succeeded in escaping ... When recaptured, particularly in France and the islands, the prisoners were given very hard sentences. In addition to the beatings on recapture they would be sentenced to 25 to 50 lashes a month and to three months solitary confinement in one of the prison dungeons on 200 grammes (less than half a pound) of bread a day and no other food. Stealing was another method of staying alive. This consisted of digging up a few potatoes and eating them raw or sneaking away to the shore to find mussels or winkles. Occasionally a German foodstore would be raided and food stolen. Those who did not steal died, which accounts for the large proportion of deaths (over 50% in Alderney, 40% in Jersey).'

'Why the Germans should have allowed such a high proportion of workers doing essential work for them to die was answered by the informants as follows: "We were treated worse than cattle. Our term of usefulness was generally accepted by the Germans as being six months. After that we were expended. They tried to get out of us every ounce of labour and energy they could on as little food as possible. If we managed to carry on for another few months well and good, and if not all went to schedule.'

This explanation is not altogether complete for, though it is true that when a Russian prisoner fell ill hardly any medical assistance was given to him, beyond placing him in a separate barrack and excusing him from work — however when 800 workmen on Alderney and 600 on Jersey were too exhausted to work, they were all sent away for a prolonged rest. At St Mâlo and at Cherbourg, exhausted Russian prisoners were given three to four months improved food and no work to enable them to recover their strength. Thereupon they were sent back to work. Furthermore several of the informants were gashed or maimed by German guards. Some of these were taken to hospital for treatment and were operated on by German doctors. In at least three instances men were sent to Paris for a further operation, yet, while taking this amount of trouble over the injured, no measures were at any time taken against the guards who crippled the workers and caused this extra work for the German medical organisation. *'The explanation according to*

some of the informants is that the cases quoted are the exception and not the rule, and that a few German doctors were sufficiently humane to take an interest in the Russian prisoners does not affect the huge proportion of deaths. Moreover, if a short treatment can revitalise sturdy workers there is no reason why they should not be treated for a certain period so that they may be further exploited.'

Political prisoner Odd Nansen remembers not being very impressed with the work of the OT volunteers:

'When one sees them at it, one realises that the result can be no great shakes, either for quantity or quality. After a closer look at their tools, one understands even more. Most things in the first place, they haven't got. There are no decent hammers. All they have are some things like Lilliputian sledgehammers. None of the axes have an edge and whetstones are unobtainable. There are no decent joiner's tools. Everything is the cheapest kind of Nuremberg trash, as we called it in the old days. It's ordered and delivered by the bundle. We saw it lying in open railway trucks in Trondheim and elsewhere. A percentage of it was ruined, rusty or smashed. There is a shortage of decent nails. They have only certain sizes which they have to make do with. But above all they are short of decent material. Round, crooked logs and the cheapest kind of building material are all that can be had. These we had to fetch from old abortive snow-shelters that are being pulled down on other hills not far away. Presumably they are last winter's abortive attempts to keep the road open. This year they'll try again. I hardly think it will come off. According to a report they are planning to build 21km of snow-roofs in all. An Oslo firm has it in hand. Perhaps we will be put on it as well.'

Prisoners of War

POWs of various nationalities were also used to supplement the labour pool, which was welcomed by some prisoners as they received extra rations. However, among the POWs who were required to work, some were very badly treated; others survived because of their inner discipline. One such group were French colonial troops—Senegalese, Moroccan, Tunisian and Algerian—some of whom had the advantage of receiving Red Cross parcels, containing cigarettes, which put them very high up, if not at the top, of the bartering ladder. 'In Jersey,' records Michael Ginns, 'thanks to the tight discipline of the senior NCO, Sergeant Mohamed ben Mohamed, described as a "true soldier of France", all 115 of them survived to return to France in 1945.' These POWs had worked on the docks and in fatigue parties in ammunition and fuel dumps, rather than actually building fortifications, and that probably holds good for most POWs everywhere.

Locals

The Germans were not averse to compelling local people to work on the Atlantic Wall, and Rommel advocated it in some cases. However, he was quick to point out that civilians worked better if they were paid promptly and in cash. This was not the case in the Netherlands, when Rotterdam and Den Haag (The Hague) became a fortress area. In May 1944 a large number of the citizens of Rotterdam were forced to work at Hoek van Holland on the fortifications, under the supervision of German soldiers. Thousands of people had been forced to move out of the densely inhabited coast zone and many of the buildings in the zone were deliberately wrecked. This caused great unrest, especially when rumours circulated that a 50km belt of fortifications was to be constructed in the coastal area. Fortunately, this proved to be exaggerated but the destruction and misery caused by the evacuations and the enforced labour were bad enough.'

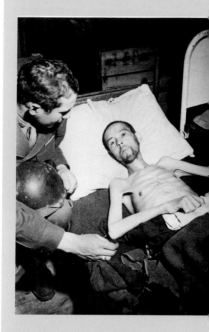

Liberated, suffering from malnutrition and tuberculosis, a Russian forced labourer is examined by a US Army doctor. The Third Reich's wartime economy was substantially boosted by the abduction of workers from conquered countries—around 12 million were taken from some 20 European countries. Most of these labourers came from Eastern Europe. Between 22 June 1941 and the end of the war, it is estimated that 5.7 million members of the Red Army fell into German hands. Of these, 3,300,000 (57.5 percent of the total) perished.

The Fortifications

German military culture was dedicated to the offensive, but understood that defensive fortifications were necessary, allowing a particular line to be held by a relatively smaller force than would otherwise be necessary. 'Economy of force', therefore, was their fundamental principle: fortifications existed not to protect their soldiers, but rather to enable them to fight more effectively and by doing so, tying down fewer men to static defence, so that the bulk of their forces could still manoeuvre. (Although, as was seen in Normandy, however, arguments over where the immediate counter-attack forces, that is to say the panzer manoeuvre force, would be located, led to major problems and contributed to Allied success.)

Atlantic Wall fortifications were broadly grouped into five categories: the smallest was the *Widerstandsnest*—pocket of resistance; next came the *Stützpunkt*—the strongpoint. These WN and StP locations were numbered, although the updating and improvement programme meant added locations and therefore renumbering. In the summer of 1942, to ensure that locations were readily identifiable, they were named either with people's or animal's names, the names reflecting whether they were under Heer, Kriegsmarine or Luftwaffe control.

The WN and StP locations were grouped into *Stützpunktgruppe*—group of strongpoints. Larger areas—usually a city or important military facility—were termed *Verteidigungsbereich* (defense area) and when grouped further these could form a fortress (*Festung*), although this term had other connotations as seen in Directive 40. Each of these levels of fortification was made up of a number of smaller units, often based around designated bunkers designed to house specific weaponry—mortars, machine guns, anti-tank weapons, artillery, etc.

In March 1945, the US War Department produced an updated version of its *Handbook on German Military Forces* (TM-E 30-451), which was issued to US troops who would be serving in Northwest Europe. Chapter V dealt specifically with 'Fortifications and Defenses'. The chapter starts with a discussion of the German organisation of the defence—three zones:

forward, main and rear allowing defence in depth. It goes on to examine the siting of defences—providing weakest terrain with strongest defences; the principle of effect before cover—ie that wide, interlocking fields of fire are more important than concealment. It covers the use of field works and obstacles—such as dragon's teeth, minefields, wire and open gun positions. Finally, it identifies the German practice to provide shelter for troops both in front line and rear positions, so that reserves can be brought up without attrition, and the importance of communications between the defence works. Next it examines the characteristics of the German fortifications:

'*1. Principles of design*
Fire effect has first priority; natural concealment is used as much as possible by blending positions with the surrounding terrain. Personnel and supply shelters, in the construction of which fire effect need not be taken into consideration, are completely below ground level, or as low as the water-table level permits. In order to present as small a target as possible to high-angle fire and bombing, emplacements, pillboxes, and casemates are built no larger than necessary to permit crews to operate their guns.

2. Construction
a. GENERAL. All permanent, fortress-type works and many field works are of concrete reinforced with steel. Some field works, however, are of masonry, brick, or timber. Steel also is used in concrete structures for beams, turrets, cupolas, gun shields, machine-gun loopholes, and doors. These installations are prefabricated and are assigned code or model numbers. The concrete works themselves are designated by type number and are constructed from plans prepared in the Army Ordnance Office.
b. THICKNESS OF CONCRETE. The usual thickness of concrete walls and roofs is 6 feet 6 inches (2 meters); smaller thicknesses are found as a rule only in the small field works. In casemates the minimum thickness of the walls and roof is 6 feet 6 inches, and generally increases commensurately with the caliber of the gun.
c. REINFORCEMENT OF CONCRETE. Most German concrete fortifications are reinforced with steel bars running in three dimensions to form cubes of 10 or 12-inch sides. ...'

Types of Fortification
In 1933 the OKH published the Order for the Construction of Permanent Fortifications (*Vorschrift zum Bau ständiger Befestigungsanlagen*) which moved toward standardisation of the works, in particular the thickness of the construction, and the armoured (*Panzerungsteilen*) and ventilation (*Lüftungsteilen* or *ML-Teile*) components. There were many developments over the next decade, especially during the construction of the Westwall, so that, when the construction of Atlantic Wall began, Organisation Todt had a portfolio of standard forms that could be used to conform with the requirements of the location.

The original Westwall bunkers were of the 100 series; as construction of the Atlantic Wall began, the 400 and 500 series came in; latterly these were improved by the 600 series. In the end there were more than 700 of the *Regelbau* (standard build) types, although many of these were relatively rare and there were many SK—*Sonderkonstruction* (special or custom-built)—types that were either adaptations of Regelbau bunkers or completely new, and many Vf locations that had little or no concrete protection.

To further complicate recognition, each of the arms of the Wehrmacht had its own range of bunkers—those suffixed "R" being for the Heer; "M" for the Kriegsmarine ("FL","V" and "S" were also used for sub-types); and "L" for the Luftwaffe. A full list can be found on the excellent http://www.bunkerinfo.nl.

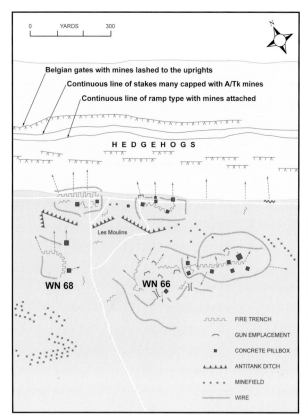

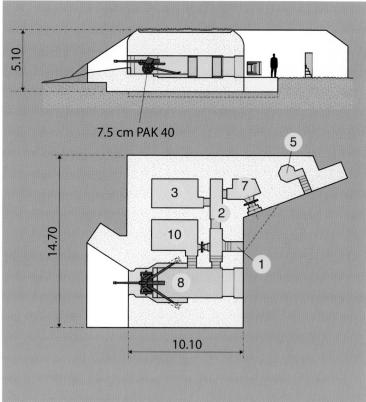

7.5 cm PAK 40

FIRE TRENCH
GUN EMPLACEMENT
CONCRETE PILLBOX
ANTITANK DITCH
MINEFIELD
WIRE

Belgian gates with mines lashed to the uprights
Continuous line of stakes many capped with A/Tk mines
Continuous line of ramp type with mines attached

HEDGEHOGS

Les Moulins

WN 68   WN 66

Above: *The defensive layout around the D-3 Les Moulins Draw on Omaha Beach exemplifies the interlocking of defensive positions. WN66 was fortified with an unfinished bunker for a 50mm gun, two heavy grenade launcher Tobruks and a 50mm gun on the bluff. Between WN66 and 68 there was an anti-tank ditch and a concrete wall sealed off the road leading up the draw where WN67 saw a Nebelwerfer emplacement for Nebelwerfer Abteilung 84, although it had no projectiles on D-Day. On the other, western, side of WN66, was WN68 armed with a Tobruk with PzKpfwIV turret, two Tobruks with Renault turrets, a 50mm gun emplacement and a concrete structure on the bluff with two gun slits.*

Above Right: *Type 625 flanking bunker showing typical arrangement with entrance (**1**) protected by an MG in the close-combat room (**7**); gaslock (**2**) opening onto the crew room (**3**) with the ammunition storage (**10**) and gun room (**8**) alongside. Note list of key numbers at the top of page 35.*

Pillboxes, casemates and other defence works were all camouflaged, where possible by banks of earth at the sides and on top, by careful siting, and the use of camouflage netting..

The Atlantic Wall bunkers had a number of consistent features as exemplified by the images that accompany this section. They are also well highlighted on the *http://regelbau.com* site (see p190) which identifies, amongst other important features:

1. Entrance—usually an armoured door defended by small-arms or MG embrasures protected by steel plates and sometimes by a dedicated *Eingangsverteidigungsscharte* (exterior flanking entrance defence loophole) coming off a close-combat room (*Nahkampfraum*). The embrasures were often shaped as an inverted step-pyramid and lined with wood to prevent ricochet bullets from entering the bunker. The doors are of armoured steel with gastight rubber seals.
2. Armored air intakes.
3. Internal insulation to reduce spalling caused by direct hits and vibration—wood wall linings and asphalt tiles.
4. Gas protection—unnecessary as it happened, but after its use in WW1 an essential precaution. Gas proofing was achieved by creating an 'over pressure' in the bunker, the air pressure higher than that outside. There was also a *Gasschleuse* (gaslock), at the entry point.
5. Emergency exit—not always there, but when included often hidden behind metal bars, brick walls and a gravel-filled stepladder tunnel.
6. Living facilities—a stove for heating (the chimney pipe had a trap so that hand grenades ended outside the bunker); a toilet.
7. Retractable periscope.
8. Armoured cupolas—found on artillery observation posts, some mortar bunkers, machine-gun or anti-tank gun emplacements.

In general terms, the bunkers built for the Atlantic Wall can be divided into

· artillery emplacements and associated bunkers
· defence bunkers
· support and personnel bunkers
· Flak and searchlight bunkers

KEY TO BUNKER LINE DRAWINGS THROUGHOUT

1 Entrance with defensive
    MG
2 Gaslock
3 Ready room/crew room
4 Escape shaft/emergency
    exit
5 Tobruk
6 Store room
7 Close combat room
    and flanking entrance
    defence loophole
8 Gun room for 75mm
9 Doors
10 Ammunition storage
11 Garage
12 Communications
13 Extra ammunition
    storage, ventilation
    and radio
14 M19 automatic mortar
15 Shell room
16 Cartridge room
17 Flanking wall as
    necessary
18 To open gun position

19 Ammunition niche
20 MG firing through
    metal plate
21 Radio room
22 Work room
23 Officer's room
24 Ventilation
25 6-embrasure Scharten-
    turm (cupola)
26 Cable rolls room
27 Shelter for ATk weapon
28 Switching room
29 Loading room
30 Plotting room
31 Communications room
32 NCO room
33 Officer's room
34 Access to basement
    storage
35 Heating room
36 Computing room
37 Radio room
38 Communications room
39 Observation room
40 Rangefinder

One of four M271 (M = naval) casemates of MKB York, StP277, at Querqueville. The casemates housed 17cm SK L/40 guns. Note the slot on the right hand side of the casemate to allow the gunsight to see when the gun is fully traversed to the left. The casemate allowed 120° of traverse. NARA

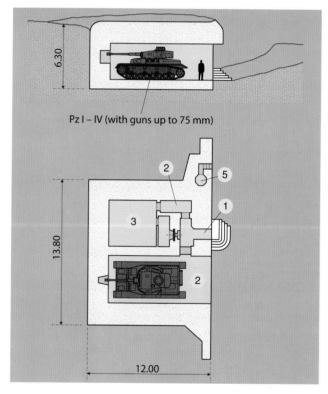

Pz I – IV (with guns up to 75 mm)

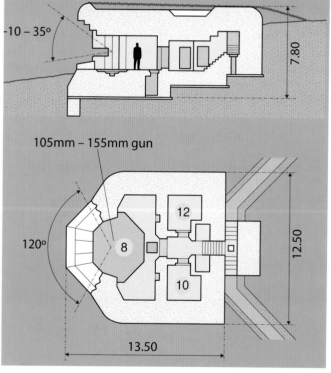

105mm – 155mm gun

Artillery

At the heavy end, many batteries were equipped with captured field artillery, most between 10 and 20cm, whose varied calibres gave the Germans significant ammunition problems. The variety also caused the Germans location problems—a range of different bunker designs was needed to accommodate different guns—and because of this variety, many of the guns were left in open emplacements or provided with "garaging"— bunkers into which the guns could be towed for protection. There was also a design to house tanks, although few were built. The efficacy of these arrangements—placing field guns in bunkers or leaving them camouflaged

Above Left: *The 602 bunker was designed to house a vehicle up to the size of a PzKpfwIV. The 603 housed two in separate rooms.*

Above: *The naval M272 bunker had a traverse of 120°. This was a popular design and was used at such batteries as Longues (near Gold Beach), Heerenduin (part of Fortress Ijmuiden) and Sperrbatterie Nord, Løkken.*

Above: *The most common defences in the Atlantic Wall were the Tobruks or Ringstände, of which there were two basic types, the Vf58c and Vf58d. Another common type was the Vf61a, housing a 50mm mortar. This had a concrete platform in the centre for supporting the mortar. Most Tobruks had a shelter behind the opening to shelter crew during a bombardment.*

in the open—was assessed by Generalleutnant Rudolf Schmetzer, who was Inspector of Land Fortifications for OB West until early 1944, and is discussed in the final chapter (see p180).

The Heer batteries tended to be inland, where open emplacements were less of a problem than on the coast, where most of the Kriegsmarine MKBs were located, often with large-calibre weapons (up to 406mm) in huge SK casemates, such as those at MKB Lindemann or Todt. There were many casemated batteries, both Heer and Kriegsmarine, along the length of the Atlantic Wall including a number that housed ships' guns (one in Norway boasted the emplaced B turret of the *Gneisenau*) and many that could have played a significant role on D-Day, such as those at Azeville, Longues, and Merville. Many of these casemated designs saw the artillery pieces removed from their usual chassis and mounted in the casemate with shields covering the opening embrasure.

All these batteries required fire control and observation posts. The Heer preferred the semicircular-fronted 636 (see drawing p114) while the Kriegsmarine range included the huge multi-storied *Marinepeilstande* in the Channel Islands. There were many observation bunkers (eg 613, 614).

Defence bunkers

The majority of casemated weapons were smaller, sited for static defence and housing the main German anti-tank weapons, from 37mm to 88mm PaK. There were a great many 47 and 50mm PaKs including the 47mm Festungspak, a bespoke piece whose barrel went through a gas-tight metal frame. There were also some bunkers for heavy mortars, the largest of which housed the 50cm M-19 Granatenwerfer. Many of these smaller artillery pieces were sited to enfilade the beaches they protected, firing from behind heavy blastwalls that protected the weapon and hid the flash when fired.

Most of the other bunkers built at the water's edge housed mortars, machine guns or flamethrowers. The most numerous of these defences were the Tobruks (so-called because of their early use in the North African campaign), the majority had a ring rail around the inside of the neck, which provided a 360° track on which to mount a machine gun. Many of the defence bunkers had armoured plating as with the PaK bunkers;

The Type 633 bunker (this one is at Oostende harbour) was equipped with an armoured turret housing an M19 50mm automatic mortar. Marc Ryckaert via WikiCommons

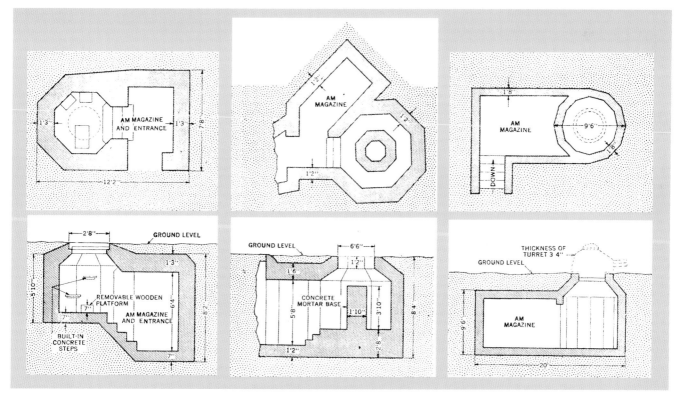

some had armoured cupolas, and some had tank turrets—often those from Renault FT (see above) or APX-Rs which mounted a 37mm anti-tank gun and a co-axial machine gun. The turret was bolted to a circular metal plate, which was rotated by hand along a 360° track, giving all-round traverse. Other obsolete tanks were also used, particularly those being dismantled for use as SP artillery chassis such as PzKpfwIIs, ex-Czech 38Ts, PzKpfw III and IVs. There were even a few Panther turrets emplaced (687) although none of the latter were used on the Atlantic Wall.

As well as individual Tobruks, many of the other bunkers had a Tobruk opening built in, accessed from outside the bunker as can be seen in the accompanying photos.

Above: *Various Tobruks, including one on the Channel Islands at Battery Dollmann (***Top Right***) mounting a Renault FT turret.*

The 600 Series

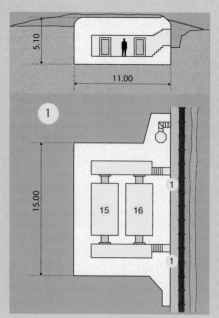

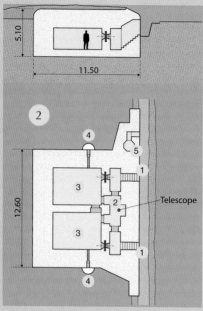

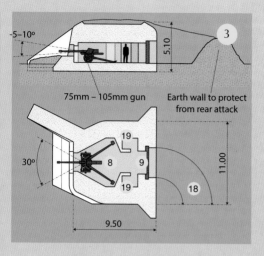

75mm – 105mm gun

Earth wall to protect from rear attack

Drawings of a variety of 600 series bunkers: 1 607; 2 622; 3 612; 4 630; 5 610; 6 634; 7 677; 8 616.

In the following list, armoured ceiling/shield indicates that the concrete has been replaced by armour plate; heavier protection indicates greater thickness of concrete; pivot-mounted means that the guns are emplaced and cannot be moved on their own carriages; flanking indicates that the bunkers have flash walls built on the side of the enemy's attack; the first degree number indicates the horizontal firing arc and the second number the vertical arc of the weapon; sea targets indicate that the weapon was intended for use against an enemy out to sea.

600 Unprotected 50mm KwK position with shelter below (6)
601 PaK shelter with armoured ceiling (6)
602 Vehicle (up to PzKpfwIV) shelter with one room (6)
603 Vehicle (up to PzKpfwIV) shelter with two rooms (12)
604 Gun shelter with one room and no embrasure (12)
605 Gun shelter with two rooms and no embrasure (12)
606 Shelter for 60cm Flak searchlight and machinery (6)
607 2-roomed ammunition shelter (0)
608 Single-level command post for Bn, Abt or Regt (6)
609 Two-level command post for Bn, Abt or Regt (23)
610 Command post for a strengthened Coy or Bty (23)
611 Casemate for field gun (60°; -9° to +35°) (0)
612 Casemate for field gun or howitzer (55° to 70°; -5° to +10°) (0)
613 Single-level Arty observation post with armoured turret (9)
614 Two-level Arty observation post with armoured turret (9)
615 Arty observation post with angled armoured ceiling (7)
616 Large comms switching station (6)
617 Comms post (9)
618 Div comms post (9)
619 Generators and machinery (0)
620 MG flanking bunker on sloping terrain with armoured shield (6)
621 Personnel shelter (10)
622 Personnel shelter (20)
623 MG flanking bunker with armoured shield (6)
624 MG flanking bunker with armoured shield and ceiling (6)
625 Flanking bunker for 7.5cm PaK 40 (6)
626 Flanking bunker for 7.5 cm PaK with armoured ceiling (6)
627 Arty observation post with armoured ceiling (7)
628 Personnel shelter (10) on sloping terrain
629 PaK shelter with concrete ceiling (6)
630 MG flanking bunker with armoured shield (6)
631 Casemate for flanking 4.7cm Festungspak (t) (7)
632 1/2 MG bunker with three-embrasured armoured turret (6)
633 Bunker for automatic M19 mortar in armoured turret (14)

634 2 MG bunker with six-embrasured armoured turret (12)
635 Personnel shelter (20) on sloping terrain
636 Fire control post (11) for an HKB (the larger 636a (14) had a sheltered roof position)
637 Fire measurement position for an HKB (3)
638 Small dressing station (5 staff; 20 wounded)
639 Large dressing station (6 staff; 20 wounded)
640 Flanking casemate for 3.7cm PaK or 4.2cm PaK 41 with armoured shield (6)
641 Ammunition shelter (weapons over 17cm) (0)
642 Bunker for 4.7 cm Festungspak (t) and MG (12)
643 1/2 MG bunker with three-embrasured armoured turret in heavier protection (6)
644 2 MG bunker with six-embrasured armoured turret in heavier protection (12)
645 Kitchen to feed up to 200 men (3)
646 Water storage for up to 7cu m of fresh water via pump or spring
647 2 MG bunker with two single-embrasured armoured turrets (9)
648 MG bunker with one single-embrasured armoured turret (6)
649 Casemate for one pivot-mounted 10.5cm gun (90°; -8° to +35°) (9)
650 Casemate for one pivot-mounted 10.5cm gun (120°; -8° to +35°) (9)
651 Casemate for one pivot-mounted 10.5cm gun (90°; -8° to +35°) without readiness room
652 Casemate for one pivot-mounted 10.5cm gun (120°; -8° to +35°) without readiness room
653 Flanking casemate for one pivot-mounted 5cm KwK (60°; -9° to +15°) (6)
654 Flanking casemate for one pivot-mounted 5cm KwK (60°; -9° to +15°) without readiness room
655 Bunker for 6 men (guncrew) and ammunition
656 Bunker for 15 men

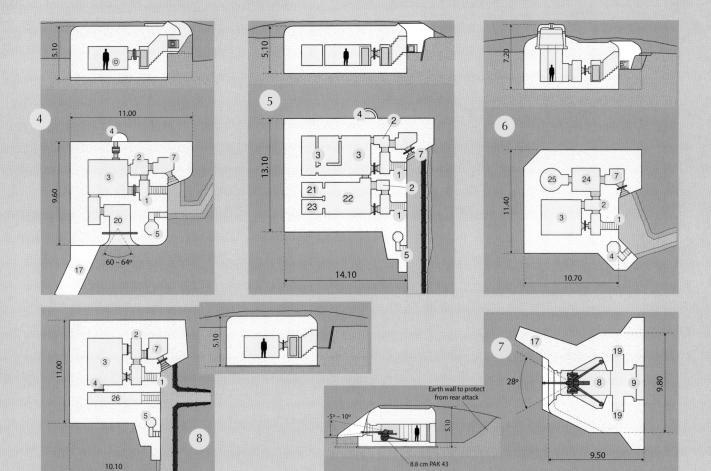

657 Shelter for 2 kitchens to feed up to 400 men (3)
658 Water storage for up to 20cu m of fresh water
659 Water storage for up to 20cu m of fresh water; heavier protection
660 Charging station (6)
661 Collection point for wounded
662 Casemate for field gun (60°; -0° to +35°) with heavier protection(9)
663 Casemate for 10 cm KK and flanking MG with heavier protection (12)—663A right-flanking MG; 663B left-flanking MG
664 Casemate for 10.5cm howitzer in turret with heavier protection (9)
665 Infantry observation bunker with armoured turret (6)
666 Infantry observation bunker with small turret (6)
667 Small flanking casemate for pivot-mounted 5 cm KwK
668 Small bunker for 6 men (could protect 20)
669 Casemate for field gun (60°; -9° to +35°) (0)
670 Casemate for pivot-mounted field gun (90°; -8° to +35°) (0)
671 Casemate for pivot-mounted field gun (120°; -8° to +35°) (0)
672 Weapon shelter with one room and no embrasure (internal space: height 2.1m x width 2.5m x length 8.35m) (0)
673 Weapon shelter with one room and no embrasure (internal space: height 2.6m x width 3m x length 9.78m) (0)
674 Small bunker for ammunition up to 10cm (0)
675 Water bunker (capacity containers for 10–13cu m) (0)
676 Small casemate for flanking 4.7cm Festungspak (t) (0)
677 Small casemate for 8.8cm PaK 43/41 (0)
678 Casemate for weapon on heavy pivot mounting (60°; -5° to +35°) (0)
679 Casemate for weapon on heavy pivot mounting (120°; -5° to +35°) (0)
680 Casemate for flanking 7.5cm PaK 40 (65°; -5° to +15°) (0)
681 Casemate for flanking MG with armoured plate (0)
682 Electrical bunker
683 Casemate for pivot-mounted 21cm gun (120°; -4° to +45°)

with heavier protection; sea targets (0)
684 Casemate for pivot-mounted 21cm gun (90°; -4° to +45°) with heavier protection; sea targets (0)
685 Casemate for pivot-mounted 21cm gun (60°; -4° to +45°) with heavier protection; sea targets (0)
686 Casemate for pivot-mounted 19.4cm 485/585 (f) gun (120°; -5° to +35°); sea targets (0)
687 Stand for Panther turret (3)
688 Casemate for 17cm Kanone on SK-L VIII mounting (120°; 0° to +45°) with heavier protection; sea targets (0)
689 Casemate for 17cm Kanone on SK-L VIII mounting (120°; -8° to +35°) with heavier protection; sea targets (0)
690 Casemate for 17cm Kanone on SK-L VIII mounting (90°; -8° to +35°) with heavier protection; sea targets (0)
691 Higher staff radio post (9)
692 Casemate for pivot-mounted 7.62cm or 8.8 cm Flak (r) (120°; 0° to +45°) with heavier protection; sea targets (0)
693 Communications bunkers using Lichtsprech und Blink-gerät (693A back to enemy; 693B front to enemy)
694 Casemate for pivot-mounted gun (120°; -3° to +35°); sea targets (0)
697 Small supplementary fire measurement position for an HKB or MKB (2)
698 Casemate for pivot-mounted 15cm 408 (i) gun (120°; 0° to +35°); sea/land targets (0)
699 Casemate for flanking 8.8cm PaK 43 (60°; -8° to +10°) (0)
700 Casemate for flanking 7.5cm PaK 40 with armoured ceiling plate (65°; -5° to +15°) (0)
701 PaK shelter with one room and no embrasure (internal space: height 2.2m x width 2.7m x length 9.6m) (0)
702 Personnel bunker without gas seal (10)
703 Casemate for flanking pivot-mounted 8.8cm PaK 43 (60°; -8° to +13°) (0)
704 Casemate for flanking pivot-mounted PaK or KwK (60°; -11° to +15°) (0)

The Atlantic Wall in the area Ob.West as of March 1, 1944 (see caption below)

R-No	BUILT	BUILDING	R-No	BUILT	BUILDING	R-No	BUILT	BUILDING
117	50	4	620	6	2	652	5	2
119	25		621	1,304	24	653	13	
120	31	2	622	1,167	39	654	5	
121	7	1	623	15	2	655	15	3
134	377	11	624	15	2	656	39	12
142	4		625	63	4	657	5	
151	46	3	626	17	11	658	20	2
246	55		627	28	2	660	1	
505	37		628	36	2	661	15	2
515	99	1	629	118	3	663		3
600	83		630	290	7	664	3	
601	28	3	631	110	2	665	1	1
602	2		632	6	2	666	2	
603	1		633	51	1	667	114	143
604	48	1	634	122	2	668	131	119
605	7		635	29	3	669	98	260
606	14	2	636	46	4	670	5	24
607	208	4	637	33		671	90	174
608	94	9	638	25	2	672	3	5
609	6		639	64	6	673	1	2
610	56	1	640	2		674	15	26
611	80	8	641	1		675	14	6
612	79	287	642	4		676	16	19
613	12	2	643	7	1	677	38	64
614	3	1	644	23	3	679	2	13
615	4		645	9	1	680	25	64
616	24		646	32	3	681	17	7
617	16		648	5	2	682	1	1
618	14		649	4				
619	5	2	650	16				

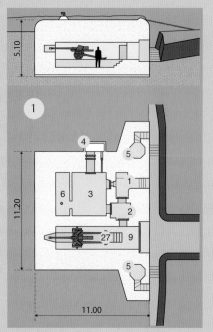

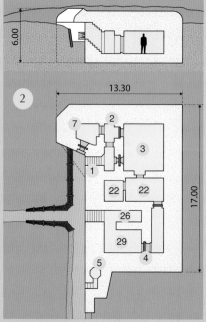

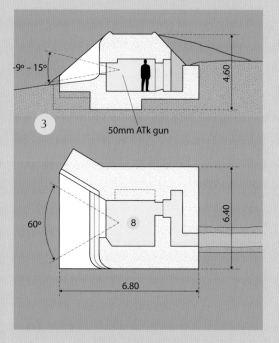

50mm ATk gun

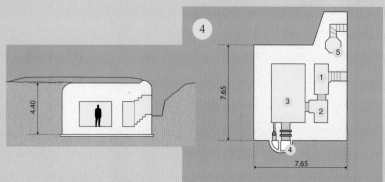

*Drawings of a variety of 600 series bunkers:
1 629; 2 617; 3 667; 4 668; 5 671; 7 669.
Within the area from the Spanish/French border
to the island of Schiermonnikoog in the West
Frisians, some 15,000 bunkers were intended.
However, by June 1944 only about two-thirds
(10,300) had been completed, with a further 800
still under construction.*

1 Shelters

Total personnel shelters	2,771	205
Total weapons and equipment	194	13
Total ammo bunkers	654	45
Total supply bunkers	190	25
SK	29	
Kriegsmarine	214	24
Air defence	190	7
Flak	112	
Other buildings	610	47
TOTALS	4,964	366

2 Reporting stations

Total reporting stations	59	
Kriegsmarine	11	4
Air defence	26	9
Other buildings	104	8
TOTALS	200	21

3 Command Posts

Total command posts	231	10
SK	5	
Kriegsmarine	99	12
Air defence	73	13
Other buildings	111	9

B Observation posts

Total infantry posts	3	1
Total artillery posts	164	11
Kriegsmarine	14	3
Air defence	74	10
Other buildings	41	10

3 Emplacements

Total MG with armoured plate	442	21
Total M.G. in armoured turrets	163	8
Total for M19 automatic mortar	51	1
Total for PaK	312	194
Total for KwK	215	143
Total for guns on mountings	257	555
Total for duns on SKL mountings	122	213
Total for KK	0	3
Total for light H.-turrets	3	0
SK	94	9
Kriegsmarine	105	73
Air defence	409	12
Other buildings	242	114

4 Heaviest guns

28cm guns	9	5
40.5cm guns	3	
Other buildings	2	3

5 Gun emplacements

7.5cm–10.5cm	220	20
15cm–20cm	236	15
22cm–24cm	20	5
Flak to 8.8 cm	138	4
Other emplacements	205	5

1 Shelters	5,683	431
2 Observation posts	296	35
3 Emplacements	2415	1,346
4 Heaviest guns	14	8
5 Gun emplacements	795	49
GRAND TOTAL	9,203	1,869

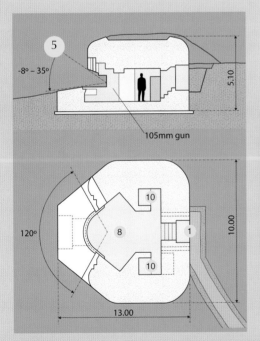

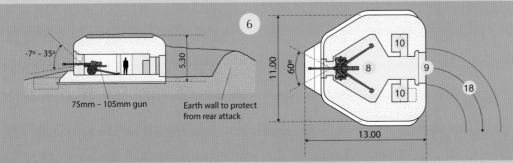

Above: *Norway has a wonderful selection of preserved bunkers. Here is an 671 at HKB 22./978 Varnes Fyr complete with original 10.5cm K332 (f). Visible above is the SK Leitstand. Petr Podebradsky*

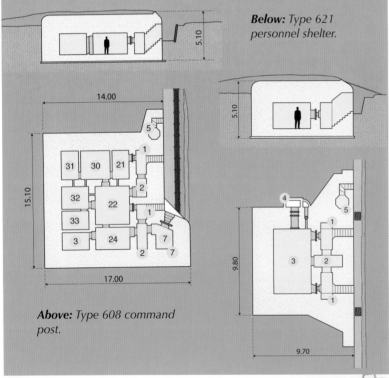

Below: Type 621
personnel shelter.

14.00

5.10

15.10

31 30 21

32 22

33

3 24

17.00

5

1

2

1

2

7

7

2

Above: Type 608 command
post.

5.10

4

5

1

3 2

1

9.80

9.70

Support and personnel bunkers

It was clearly desirable to have adequate shelters for all troops manning the fortifications, and the bulk of the Atlantic Wall bunkers were constructed to protect personnel and equipment. Generally they were built in the rear of the fortified line to house reserves and also in individual defensive positions to house troops manning installations. The main personnel shelters had room for two sections (502/622 roughly 20 men), or 10 men in one shelter (501/621); others were designed for 15 (656) and 6 (668)—although the latter could protect 20 during a bombardment. Personnel shelters could also be used as medical stations or signal centres. However, the types provided specially for such purposes had differing designs, size and number of interior compartments and other modifications as can be seen from the final section in this chapter looking at the Regelbau 600 series.

Other support bunkers were required for kitchens (645, 657), ammunition (607, 641, 674)—not all the bunkers had space for the ammunition they'd have to expend—and water storage (668, 669, 675), and to provide shelters and medical facilities for the wounded (638, 639, 661).

Command and Communications

While defensive weapons and troop safety were obviously significant at the front, command and control was of paramount importance. The *Leitstände* of the Heer and the *Marinepeilstände* controlled the fire of batteries; control of *Bataillone*, *Abteilungen*, and *Regimenten* was also emplaced in bunkered command posts (608, 609, 610).

Radar/communication bunkers

The Normandy coast was known to the Germans as the "Signal Coast" because so many radio locating and ranging stations had been installed there. Air defence radar was in its infancy during World War II and there were a number of different systems: the Germans used Freya and the larger derivatives Mammut, Wasserman and Jagdschloss. Fighter control used the Würzburg and larger Riese Würzburg. Other types include Elefant (in the Netherlands and See-Elefant off Denmark and the fascinating Klein Heidelberg bistatic radar stations linked into Luftwaffe L480 bunkers. Many of the bunkers that housed this sort of equipment are the largest within the Luftwaffe types.

Flak

At the beginning of the war nearly a million men — almost two-thirds of the total Luftwaffe manpower — was serving in the flak arm. Its size increased so that by summer 1944 there were some million and a quarter men and women, that is to say nearly half of the Luftwaffe, so employed. Basic flak units were of four types—heavy, light, mixed and searchlight—and they were to be found all along the Atlantic Wall, sometimes with the dual purpose of being able to engage naval targets as well as aircraft. Of course, as with the Heer, many sailors and airmen were in a supporting role; for example, Hans Speidel says that there were more than 300,000 Luftwaffe personnel making up the ground staff of the Luftwaffe in the west alone, which worked out to 100 ground staff for every airman. Bitterly he ascribes this position to the 'ambition of Göring to create a special force of his own—a peculiar urge that seizes the grandees of any revolution.'

The navy had their own Flak units to protect their installations. In addition to the searchlights used on aircraft, the Kriegsmarine also had

Above and Opposite: *The 621 housed 10 men and was one of the mainstays of the Atlantic Wall. This one—StP Brück, WN c—is near Calais-Dunkerque airport at Les Hemmes.*

Opposite: *The Hillman strongpoint (WN17) above Colleville-Montgomery housed the command post for the area. It has two Type 608 bunkers. This one has had a cupola added.*

searchlights to illuminate targets on the sea. There were standarized bunkers for most of the common Flak weapons and these bunkers had ammo and personnel shelters, with gun emplacements on the roof set up so they could be used in ground and AA roles. Others are mainly for command posts and radars.

Other Defences

Anyone who has studied the D-Day landings will know about the range of defences that were used. Many of the obstacles used on the Atlantic Wall—such as anti-tank ditches, concrete 'dragon's teeth' of various types, anti-tank walls, and barbed-wire entanglements—were standard German field engineering obstacles that could be found in other locations such as on the Westwall. However, the Atlantic Wall, as it covered the coast, had numerous obstacles designed to slow down and indefinately hinder an amphibious landing. These were of particular importance to Rommel, indeed, in Schmezer's debriefing document he mentions the foreshore specifically:

'besides the examination and improvement of the all-round defenses of all strong points, and of the obstacles on the beach, there was finally the important task of constructing off-shore obstacles (also carried out by a great effort by the units of the Organization Todt and urgently demanded by Field Marshal Rommel), with a deep zone of water obstacles against enemy landing craft was to be created along all strips of coast endangered by landing operations, and which obstacles were to be effective during both low and high tide.'

Obstacles were usually erected within main battle positions, covered by fire from open emplacements or pillboxes and could be either fixed or movable. They were generally made of steel and concrete, but Rommel also incorporated wooden obstacles.

Mention should also be made of two other significant hazards to an invader: the use of flooding—particularly in low lying areas of France and the Netherlands—and the attempts made to restrict glider landing zones, often by using 'Rommel's asparagus', metal or wooden poles that studded the fields.

Minefields

Normally laid to a definite pattern, except in areas where the German commanders did not wish to undertake offensive action, where they might well be sewn irregularly. Within an anti-tank minefield there would generally also be some anti-personnel mines, so as to make the job of clearing a gap more hazardous. The reverse was also used, namely a row or two of anti-tank mines would be laid on the edge of an anti-personnel minefield, so that an AFV could not just drive through detonating the anti-personnel mines. Safe lanes would be left through minefields, to allow for patrolling. and these were varied from time to time. Mines would generally be laid close to or on roads, railways, airfields and at other important points. Hastily scattered mines might well be used on surfaced roads when time did not permit digging them in. German mines were generally of excellent quality; for example, the Teller anti-tank mine (the basic Tmi 29 contained 4.5kg of TNT) and the Schuminen (universally known as S-mines) were lethal anti-personnel mines.

In *The History of Landmines*, Mike Croll cites the situation which pertained in Guernsey as being something of a 'microcosm of German mine warfare'. Here, postwar, the clearance of the small (approximately 90 sq km) island involved lifting a total of 115 minefields, containing a staggering 72,866 mines, including Teller mines, S-mines, *Stockminen* (stake mines) and locally made versions of the S-mine. He goes on to explain how:

'Large areas of the island were planted with 'Rommel's Asparagus', using captured French 300lb shells and much of the coastline featured mined underwater obstacles. Along the cliffs 518 improvised mines and over 1000 Rollbomben [aircraft bombs] were used.'

These last were aircraft bombs placed on top of the cliffs and camouflaged, which could then be rolled down on top of anyone climbing up!

Above: *Clearing minefields was a long and dangerous job. Eric Bates remembers being taken from his AA battery to go to Calais to lift mines. He—and many other single men— was chosen because he had volunteered to do the mine-clearing training in the UK before D-Day.* NARA

Left: *Goliath was a small remotely controlled demolition tank, which was filled with high explosive. It could be used against tanks, pillboxes and such like.*

Below Left: *Beaches were protected by mines on stakes and a variety of metal and timber structures designed to hinder landing craft.*

Opposite, Top and Centre Above: *Flak positions were sited along the Atlantic Wall, particularly near important batteries or other defensive positions.* NARA

Opposite, Centre Below: *Strongpoints included barbed-wire entanglements even in towns.* NARA

Opposite, Bottom: *Miles of reinforced-concrete anti-tank walls were built at key choke points or on beach landing draws.* NARA

2 ENTER ROMMEL

Opposite, Left: *Rommel in Denmark. General der Infanterie Hermann von Hanneken next to him was commander of the German forces in Denmark from 29 September 1942 to January 1945. He was replaced by Georg Lindemann after a court-martial had found him guilty of corruption.*

It was now time for one of Germany's most famous soldiers to play his part in the saga of the Atlantic Wall. Generalfeldmarschall Erwin Johannes Eugen Rommel had made his name in France in 1940. In North Africa he became the 'Desert Fox', a legendary panzer leader and military hero: his qualities included brilliant leadership and outstanding tactical ability, combined with his realisation that showmanship was equally important to becoming a successful commander. He was someone who was admired—even almost revered—by the enemy as well as by his own troops. Despite sickness and eventual defeat in North Africa, he was still one of the brightest stars of the Wehrmacht.

On leaving North Africa, he had been earmarked by Hitler for a senior position in Italy, as C-in-C Armeegruppe B. In the end Hitler decided to give Kesselring complete charge in Italy and to find Rommel and his burgeoning new HQ another task. OKW was in favour of disbanding Armeegruppe B, but as von Rundstedt's chief of staff, Gunther Blumentritt, explained, Hitler had other ideas:

'Against this Hitler ordered its [HQ Armeegruppe B] revival. He knew that in 1944 something vital would occur in the west or on some other front and on that account wished to hold this valuable staff in reserve. But in order to keep Rommel and his staff employed until a responsible position could be found for him somewhere, Hitler decided to entrust him with the inspection of western defences.'

Hitler gave Rommel vague instructions based on his Führer Directive 51. OKW later confirmed to OB West (von Rundstedt) their outline content. Basically Hitler's aims in appointing Rommel were threefold:

1. So that Rommel could familiarise himself with that sector of the Western Front which would undoubtedly prove to be the decisive one, namely the Channel coast area.
2. To have Rommel take all necessary steps to rectify any shortcomings in the Atlantic Wall defences, making full use of the OT and other resources.
3. To avail himself of Rommel's experience in fighting the Allies, in particular the British.

Below: *Rommel and Hitler. For a while Hitler's favourite general, Rommel, however, was implicated in the reprisals following 20 July bomb plot, and was forced to commit suicide.*

Rommel had authority to report directly to Hitler, which inevitably led to friction, not so much between the two field marshals or between their two headquarters—OB West and Armeegruppe B—but rather in departmental circles and in their relations with the Luftwaffe's Luftflotte 3 and the Kriegsmarine's Naval Fleet West, both of whom had their own distinct lines of communication up to OKW.

So Rommel took off from Villafranca airfield on 21 November 1943 bound for the close bocage country of Normandy through which his 'road to fame' had passed in the heady days of 1940. Now he was *Inspekteur der Küstenverteidigung* (Inspector of Coastal Defence) and would prove to everyone that he had an inbuilt sixth sense when it came to spotting the unspottable, plus a talent for inventing obstacles

second to none and, above all, the ability to impress almost anyone with his enthusiasm and sheer common sense.

Rommel had begun assembling his inspection team while he was still in Italy. Acting on the advice of his then chief of staff, Generalmajor Alfred Gause—one of his trusted Afrikaners—he requested the assignment of Vizeadmiral Friedrich Oskar Ruge as the team's Naval Liaison Officer (*Marineverbindungsoffizier*). Soon after his arrival, Rommel sent Ruge off to see the Kriegsmarine staff in Berlin and to collect as much background material as he could that would help them with their task—such items as tide tables, maps and charts, shipping details and other maritime information. He would return to rejoin the team whilst they were en route—actually rejoining Rommel in northern Jutland on 2 December. It was indeed fortunate that Ruge had a detailed personal knowledge of the coast, because much of the material that he so painstakingly collected was destroyed in an air-raid when he was still in Berlin.

A special train had been arranged for the team, with spacious apartments and a 'parlour car' which Ruge reckoned had been designed for a Balkan potentate. There was also a large briefing room and a dining car. The team boarded the train on 1 December at Munich railway station bound for Copenhagen, where the inspection tour would begin with a visit to General Hermann von Hanneken, who commanded all the German forces in Denmark. Rommel met him on the evening of 2 December and began his tour the next morning at Esbjerg on the west coast of Jutland. They spent ten days in Denmark, in which short time Rommel realised that the much-vaunted Atlantic Wall was a hollow sham and that a vast amount of work would be needed if a determined enemy assault was to be defeated. He was soon to discover that this applied to most of the rest of these supposedly impregnable defences. Rommel also realised that they were planning to fight the main battles too far back from the coast. He had already decided upon his main strategy, namely that the Allies must be defeated on the beaches before they could gain a proper foothold and he would propound this message over and over again. In his logical way he reasoned that mobile warfare—of which he was master—would be impossible against an enemy with total air superiority and a vast preponderance of mechanised weapons—tanks, guns, vehicles—at their disposal.

'I consider therefore that an attempt must be made, using every possible expedient, to beat off the enemy landing on the coast and to fight the battle in the more or less strongly fortified coastal strip.'

Generalfeldmarschall Erwin Rommel and Vizeadmiral Friedrich Ruge visiting the U-Boot bunkers at La Rochelle, 12 February 1944. Ruge was a jovial Swabian and, as Rommel also hailed from Swabia, there was an immediate rapport. He soon became a firm and trusted friend to whom Rommel could talk frankly. He had entered the Kriegsmarine in 1914, served in the Baltic and led destroyer raids on Britain. In 1920 he had begun specialising in mine warfare and also established a reputation as a military writer. Ruge arrived on 30 November. 'I reported in this irregular attire,' he wrote later referring to his warm and unmilitary muffler; 'but it seemed unimportant, since Rommel was apparently less interested in the uniform than in the man inside it. Rommel appeared smaller than I had imagined him, rather serious, full of energy and very natural.' Postwar Ruge became Inspector of the Bundesmarine from 1956 until he retired in 1961.

He told his chief engineer officer, General Wilhelm Meise, much the same:

'When the invasion begins our own supply lines won't be able to bring forward any aircraft, gasoline, rockets, tanks, guns or shells because of enemy air attacks. That alone will rule out any sweeping land battles. Our only possible chance will be at the beaches—that's where the enemy is always weakest.'

He would hold this view throughout his period of command of Armeegruppe B, despite the attempts of others who wanted to fight the battle differently. It was fortunate indeed for the Allies that Rommel's logical approach was not followed to the letter.

After concluding that Denmark showed, in Ruge's words, 'how overtaxed the Wehrmacht was—a handful of modestly trained and equipped static divisions had to defend hundreds of kilometres of excellent landing beach,' most of the team moved to Rommel's new headquarters at Fontainebleau. Rommel flew to southern Germany for a few days leave, then rejoined them on 18 December. The new HQ was a small luxurious chateau which had once belonged to Madame de Pompadour.

The following day he visited von Rundstedt in Paris, writing to his wife afterwards that: 'R is very charming and I think everything will go well.' There was, undoubtedly, a certain amount of mutual respect between them—von Rundstedt was, at 68, Germany's most senior soldier, with Rommel, a mere 52, its youngest field marshal. Although he perhaps saw the younger man as a threat, von Rundstedt was quite happy to let Rommel do all the work.

As his main headquarters staff began to settle into Maison Pompadour at Fontainebleau, Rommel and his inspection team continued their tour. The week before Christmas they were inspecting the most important area, namely the Channel coast, and Rommel was again extremely disturbed by all he saw—the lack of proper defences, the relatively poor quality of many of the troops who would have the task of confronting the coming invasion, and the lack of a coherent command structure. He did not break for Christmas, but continued his tours and reports.

'Out on the move a lot,' he wrote to his son Manfred, 'and raising plenty of dust wherever I go.' To his wife Lucie he wrote: 'I'm going to throw myself into this new job with everything I've got and I'm going to see it turns out a success.' So he went everywhere and saw everything—including Luftwaffe and Kriegsmarine units and their headquarters as well as those of the Heer, also the secret V-weapon sites (he visited one on Christmas Day); nowhere was excluded. His staff were appalled at the pressure under which he worked—and of course he made them work just as hard.

One of his favourite topics was the laying of mines and the planning of defensive minefields, of which he had gained much expertise in North Africa—for example, in his preparations for the Battle of El Alamein. Now he wanted to lay many, many more. He told Meise:

'I want anti-personnel mines, anti-tank mines, anti-paratroop mines. I want mines to sink ships and mines to sink landing craft. I want some minefields designed so that our infantry can cross them but not enemy tanks. I want mines that detonate when a wire is tripped; mines that explode when a wire is cut; mines that can be remotely controlled and mines that will explode when a beam of light is interrupted. Some of them must be encased in a nonferrous metal, so that the enemy's mine detectors won't register them.'

Rommel explained his plan for laying mines all the way along the coast. There were over 600,000 mines waiting to be laid, Rommel told Salmuth, that even dummy minefields had proved their worth in North Africa. Rommel and Salmuth toured the Fifteenth Army sector and visited everywhere, driving like a whirlwind through the French towns and villages in a Horch car, frequently to the shouts of 'C'est Rommel!' from the local populace.

During December and January Rommel continued his inspections, covering mile after mile of coast in tireless reconnaissance; turning out coastal battalion after coastal battalion for inspection, march-past and preemptory interrogation; quizzing commanders, from generals down to corporals, finding out their views and laying down his own priorities. He was convinced that, in most places where a landing was possible, there should be several parallel minefields, each some kilometres wide, forming a defensive zone up to 8km in depth and requiring many millions of mines. These minefields would be covered from fortified strongpoints, sometimes including stationary tanks, and requiring considerable constructional effort. Dummy positions were to be built in order to deceive the invader, whilst fictitious staffs, movement tables, orders and so forth, would be co-ordinated into an army group deception programme—not unlike what the Allies were doing on the other side of the Channel. In the sea itself would be four belts of underwater obstacles, one in 2m of water, one at low tide, one at half tide and one at mean high tide. Against airborne attack Rommel ordered the erection of stakes (soon known as 'Rommel's asparagus'). Everywhere he went he produced new ideas from his ever-fertile imagination.

Rommel continued his inspection tours for some months—he did not visit the western and southern coastlines in France until February 1944—then set about writing his report. In general he had been very disturbed by almost everything he had seen. He found the Heer forces to be 'barely adequate' for a vigorous defence, while the Kriegsmarine and Luftwaffe were both too weak to be able to provide tangible help. There was a lack of a proper defensive plan, except for the fortresses. Everywhere there was a lack of mobility and of basic defensive weapons such as minefields. 'I have ordered all the troops to rain stakes into the beaches as a barrier against landing craft,' he noted in his diary on 15 January 1944, the day on which he was given tactical command of all troops on the coast opposite Great Britain. He also made an educated guess as to where the enemy landings were most likely to take place—namely in the Pas de Calais area, because of the presence there of the V-rocket sites—although he later retracted this guess. He identified that the enemy would precede any seaborne landings with severe aerial bombing, sea bombardments and airborne landings, and that he did not think the coastal defences were strong enough to withstand the Allied attack. He emphasised that an immediate and decisive counter-attack would have to be launched and that this was the main reason for keeping mobile troops—panzers and panzergrenadiers—close to the coast. This was to be the main bone of contention with von Rundstedt and his advisors.

Rommel's Report

Completed and signed on 22 April, Rommel's report was long and detailed, containing many comments and instructions for everyone involved in manning the Atlantic Wall. He started by sugaring the pill:

'Almost without exception unusual progress has been made in all defence group sectors in accordance with the seriousness of the situation. I expressed my satisfaction to the commanders and troops of all available forces and their clever employment of a great part of the civilian population.'

Then he came to the point:

'Here and there I have noticed units that do not seem to have recognised the urgency of the situation and who do not even follow instructions.'

OB West Gerd von Rundstedt was Rommel's immediate superior. General Hans Speidel said of him:

'Rundstedt's character, personality and mobility were fading and, at a time when supreme efforts were demanded, Rundstedt remained unknown to the soldier at the front, while Rommel ceaselessly exerted his remarkable powers of leadership on the soldiers personally, sparing himself not at all.'

Von Rundstedt would deliver the eulogy to Rommel at his state funeral.

Rommel then listed examples, such as his instruction that all mines laid on the beaches had to he live all the time, but that he had found this order has heen countermanded in some locations.

'I do not intend to issue unnecessary orders every day. I give orders only when and if necessary. I expect, however, that my orders will be executed at once and to the letter and that no unit under my command makes changes, or even gives orders to the contrary, or delays execution through unecessary red tape. On the contrary, I expect that all my orders will be followed immediately and precisely and that the carrying out of orders will be supervised.'

Then he listed various conclusions he had reached, which comprised, in essence, an engineering treatise on obstacles of all types.

• **Beach Defences** In general these K obstacles (K = *Küste*—coast)) needed to be 'dense and effective' so that they would not only delay the enemy but also destroy him in the water. Rommel mentioned items such as the Nutcracker Mine I–III, the concrete shell for the Teller mine (to reduce the shock of other explosions such as shell fire setting off the mines in sympathy) and the concrete obstacles known as tetrahedra. The first of these were, according to experiments, very effective against landing craft and amphibious vehicles, including tanks. The concrete shells also protected against the penetration by seawater and the pressure of the waves which could cause the charge to detonate. Little by little, the density of mines on the beaches had to be brought up to one per metre.

Factories for concrete In every sector the factories making concrete structures needed to liaise with the OT, so as to produce the special mixtures of concrete, which the OT already knew about.

*Concrete foundations for Czech obstacles (***Tschechenigel***)*These improved the obstacles considerably by raising them up and so stopping them from becoming choked up with sand—a major threat to beach defences. Where concrete was unavailable Rommel said brushwood mats were to be used as they had already proved very effective.

Tetrahedra Steel tetrahedra were better than the lighter concrete ones. They were also particularly valuable in locations where it was impossible to drive in stakes—such as on cliffs and in shallow water. They were operated by pulleys mounted on anchored boats or floats and operated with the use of horses. Mines could be fixed to their front that would explode on contact so as to destroy enemy vessels as well as merely stopping them.

*Ram logs (***Hemmelbalker***)* These had proved very effective even against large boats, but must have a slope of 30°–40° Installing saw-like/chisel-like blades to protrude a few inches would help to cut open the bottom of a ship. Mined logs needed to be carefully and systematically placed at 20m intervals and at great depth.

*Belgian Gates (***Rollbocke *and* Hemmkueen***—also called 'Element 'C')* Like the Czech obstacles, these could be very effective against boats. 'Some units,' commented Rommel, 'even installed mines on *Rollbocke* which I advise strongly.' He also told units to alter the placing of their movable K obstacles as often as possible on the beach, but commented that: 'most units, however, have been slack in this respect'.

• **Defences against Airborne Troops** Rommel explained that he had been ordered to take charge of defences against airborne troops. He especially thanked 348th Infantry Division (in the Dieppe area) for the way it had installed—and was continuing to install—'strong obstacles against airborne troops in the sector between land and sea in such a quick and thorough manner.' The division had managed to employ civilians (including women who sang at their work) principally because it paid them immediately and in cash. The placing of logs and the wiring of open fields was of the greatest importance, because, as Rommel explained:

'The time seems to be near when the coast cannot be penetrated from the sea by amphibious units on account of the strength of the K obstacles and the fortress-like defences. Only by using numerous airborne troops as reinforcements will a seaborne assault have any chance of succeeding.'

He then explained the threat posed by these airborne and glider-borne troops, and ordered 'The thorough fencing-in of the area between land and sea is to be accomplished as quickly as possible by all divisions.'

• ***Mining*** Rommel expressed his worries that in many places mining of the coastal band of 300–10,000m had not been completed with real minefields or even covered by dummy ones, which he said could be used where mines were in short supply. He also made the point that there could be no mines in areas where farmers were ploughing or cattle grazing. Areas of major minefields were not to be taken up without Heer permission, whilst a broad minefield was to be laid around all fortress-like installations. Both the Americans and the British disliked entering potential minefields, and Rommel commented that even their experts could not tell a dummy minefield from a real one without properly checking it over. Engineers were not needed for the construction of dummy minefields except for their planning. All officers had to be able to construct dummy minefields.

• ***Camouflage of Defence Positions*** He commented that he had seen very well-constructed battle installations in the middle of green fields, yet the camouflage nets were the old-style black ones, which allowed enemy bombers to recognise them from a great height. The old nets must therefore be newly sprayed to fit in with their surroundings—or used on dummy installations.

• ***Use of Smokescreens*** The use of artificial smoke during enemy attacks was highly recommended, but using burning leaves or straw for makeshift smoke could, Rommel said, be just as effective, especially because artificial smoke was so scarce. It could also be used to draw the enemy's attention to dummy installations.

• ***Tearing Down and Mining Beach Houses*** There had been too much tearing down of houses. Rommel argued that the enemy would most likely shoot at such houses, villages and towns, if they were visible from the sea. Therefore they should only be taken down if it was necessary to create a field of fire, otherwise it was better to leave them as targets for the enemy. Mining such houses had proved unsatisfactory, and it was more effective to use mines on the beach or in minefields. Every bomb dropped or shell fired at these houses was one less to be used against the defenders.

• ***Reinforcements*** Commanders had to make use of every single man in the short time left before the enemy came and any member of the civilian population as well. He quoted an example in one company where only 13 men out of 180 were working on the beach and the rest were occupied in the bivouac area in which they had lived for over a year. Nothing had been done to protect their front lines.

• ***Co-operation between Infantry and Artillery*** This was essential and he mentioned a professional demonstration that he had watched when 'all arms had interacted with great speed and professionalism.' Such co-operation was to be encouraged, especially with the coastal naval batteries.

Hans Speidel was Rommel's chief of staff and after his boss's suicide retained the post under Günther von Kluge and Walther Model. He was implicated in the 20 July plot to assassinate Hitler, after which he was held prisoner for seven months before escaping to Allied troops. A professor of modern history postwar, he wrote Invasion 1944: Rommel and the Normandy Campaign which was published in 1950. He later returned to the military, becoming Supreme Commander of the NATO ground forces in Central Europe from 1957 to 1963. Bundesarchiv, Bild 146-2004-0024/CC-BY-SA 3.0

Conclusion

Rommel closed his report by re-emphasising that the German forces needed swiftly to bring all their defences up to such a standard that they would hold up against the strongest attacks.

'Our defences, together with the sea, represent one of the strongest defence lines in History.

'The enemy must be annihilated before he reaches our main battlefield ... From week to week the Atlantic Wall will grow stronger and the equipment of our troops manning the defences will get better. Considering the strength of our defences and the courage, ability and the determination to fight being displayed by all our soldiers, we can look forward with the utmost confidence to the day when the enemy will attack the Atlantic Wall. It will and must lead to the destruction of the attackers and that will be our contribution to the revenge we owe the English and Americans for the inhuman warfare they are waging against our homeland.'

Armeegruppe B assumes command

Meanwhile, Rommel's headquarters, Armeegruppe B, had taken over responsibility for the Channel and Atlantic coast north of the River Loire on 15 January 1944. This was the area in which Hitler was convinced that the Allies would land, as this extract from a talk the Führer gave to the C-in-Cs of the three branches of the Wehrmacht, and all the Heer and Festung commanders on 20 March 1944, shows:

'It is obvious that the Anglo-Americans will and must land in the west... The most suitable and hence most threatened areas are the two peninsulas in the west, Cherbourg and Brest, which are very tempting and offer the best possibilities for forming a beachhead.'

He went on to emphasise that it would be essential for the enemy to gain a port. The command structure put in place is shown below.

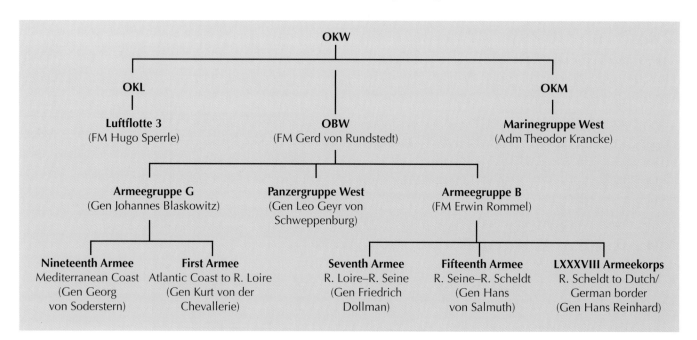

The command structure was fundamentally flawed in a number of ways. First, von Rundstedt's OB West had no direct control over the other two services. Second, Geyr von Schweppenburg's Panzergruppe West HQ, created in late January 1944, did not come under Rommel's Armeegruppe B. On top of this LXXXVIII Armeekorps—responsible for the North Sea coast, the Scheldt estuary and the Dutch/German border area—officially came

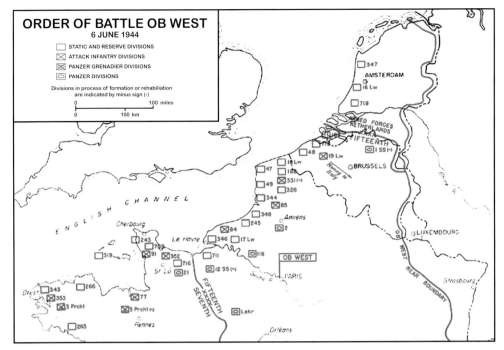

ORDER OF BATTLE OB WEST
6 JUNE 1944

☐ STATIC AND RESERVE DIVISIONS
☒ ATTACK INFANTRY DIVISIONS
⊠ PANZER GRENADIER DIVISIONS
▢ PANZER DIVISIONS

Divisions in process of formation or rehabilitation
are indicated by minus sign (-)

0 _____ 100 miles
0 _____ 100 km

under the commander of all German forces in the Netherlands (General der Flieger Friedrich Christiansen), although in practice Armeegruppe B went straight to the corps commander General Hans Reinhardt.

Rommel was unhappy with his Maison Pompadour HQ—it was far too far to the rear—so OKW assigned him the chateau at La Roche-Guyon, some 80km west of Paris, overlooking the Lower Seine and less than 130km from the coast. HQ Armeegruppe B moved into La Roche Guyon on 9 March but Rommel spent little time in his new headquarters, being constantly on the road, visiting his troops and stirring them into almost ceaseless activity. Single-minded to a fault, when one of his party remarked on the beauty of the spring flowers in the area they were visiting, Rommel is supposed to have replied, 'Make a note, this area will take at least a thousand mines!' On another occasion, when asked if he would like to visit the famous porcelain works at Sevres, he quickly agreed as he wanted to see if they could turn out waterproof casings for his sea mines. Adm Ruge lists the following as being the major problems that emerged from their inspection tours:

1. There was no unified basic concept for the defence. Some commanders in some areas were doing their best to build defences in their immediate area, but nothing had been co-ordinated.

2. Defences of the few major ports had been taken in hand according to clear plans, but not all were as yet completed. Useful information had been gained from the British raids, such as on Dieppe, where harbour protection batteries had been located outside the defensive zone and were thus easily eliminated by the enemy.

3. No agreement had been reached about the basic principles of siting coastal artillery batteries. This was never resolved in France, so coastal guns lacked the sophisticated fire control systems that were available, for example, in the Channel Islands.

4. Rommel thought that sea mines were a good way of stopping and damaging an assaulting enemy, but as the need for such mines had not been considered before, Mine Research Command was still perfecting designs.

5. There was a lack of striking power and flexibility among the troops— particularly in Denmark where there was more evidence of, as Rommel put it, the 'horse and bicycle, rather than the aircraft and the tank'.

6. Finally, the hardy annual that would never go away, the lack of co-operation between the services at the highest command level, despite

Leo Geyr von Schweppenburg commanded 3rd Pz Div in Poland, XXIV Panzerkorps in France and the invasion of the Soviet Union. In early 1943 he was ordered west to set up a Panzer/Panzergrenadier force which became Panzergruppe West on 19 November 1943. His main disagreement with Rommel, concerned the positioning of this force: Rommel wanted it as close to the coast as possible; von Schweppenburg and von Rundstedt preferrred it inland. During the invasion three panzer divisions were rushed northward and held up British and Canadian forces for a month—but von Schweppenburg had been wounded on 10 June 1944, when RAF aircraft—as a result of an Ultra intercept—attacked his headquarters at La Caine killing a number of senior officers. This forced the cancellation of the counterattack. Von Schweppenburg was relieved of his command on 2 July 1944, he ended the war as Inspector General of Armoured Troops.

the good personal relations on the ground. This led to anomalies such as siting naval batteries and air force radars in front of infantry positions which were actually there to defend them.

By the spring of 1944, Armeegruppe B comprised:
Fifteenth Armee—LXXXI, LXXXII, LXXXIX and LXVII (Reserve) Armeekorps.
Seventh Armee—initially XXV, LXXIV and LXXXIV Armeekorps, plus later II FJR Korps.
LXXXVIII Armeekorps—in the Netherlands.

As D-Day approached more reinforcements reached the divisions within these corps. Some were also refitted and regrouped, while others—mainly the reserve divisions—were still training. Another significant change was that, within the OB West area, the tank strength doubled—from 752 in early January 1944 to 1,403 by the end of April. There were in total 16 infantry and parachute divisions, ten armoured and mechanised divisions, together with 25 coastal and seven reserve divisions, making up the 58 divisions in OB West. The panzer, mechanised and parachute divisions would clearly prove to be the most difficult opposition for the assaulting forces.

Fifteenth Armee

Within the four Armeekorps there were 15 infantry divisions and three Luftwaffe field divisions: seven infantry and two Luftwaffe in the front line on the coast; eight infantry and one Luftwaffe in the hinterland. Generaloberst Hans von Salmuth, the army commander, was a highly experienced officer, who had initially received a monumental telling off from Rommel, but thereafter was one of his of strongest supporters. HQ Fifteenth Armee was located at Tourcoing. The outline organisation of Fifteenth Armee as at 6 June 1944 was (asterisks identify front-line units):

LXXXI KORPS	LXXXII KORPS	LXXXIX KORPS	LXVII KORPS
3401 Inf Div	47th Inf Div*	48th Inf Div	49th Inf Div*
245th Inf Div*	182nd Inf Div	165th Inf Div	85th Inf Div
346th Inf Div*	331st Inf Div	712th Inf Div	326th Inf Div
348th Inf Div*	18th Luftwaffe Fd Div*	19th Luftwaffe Fd Div	344th Inf Div*
711th Inf Div*			
17th Luftwaffe Fd Div*		(Additionally 70th Inf Div was on Walcheren Island)	

Seventh Armee

Rommel's other army was the Seventh and within it were three, later four, Armeekorps, containing a total of 15 divisions. The army commander was a highly experienced artilleryman, Generaloberst Friedrich Dollmann. However, he died in his HQ at Le Mans of a heart attack on 29 June 1944, just two days after the loss of Cherbourg. Rommel wished to promote General der Artillerie Erich Marcks, then the very able commander of LXXXIV Korps, who was immediately available within Seventh Army, but Hitler did not approve him for political reasons. Instead he chose Obergruppenführer der Waffen-SS Paul Hausser, then commanding II SS Panzerkorps, to replace Dollmann. It was to be the forward units of Marcks' LXXXIV Korps which would face the initial Allied onslaught. On 6 June 1944, the outline organisation of the Seventh Armee was:

XXV KORPS	LXXIV KORPS	LXXXIV KORPS	II FJR KORPS
265th Inf Div	77th Inf Div	243rd Inf Div	91st Air Landing Div**
275th Inf Div	266th Inf Div	319th Inf Div*	2nd Parchute Div**
343rd Inf Div	353rd Inf Div	352nd Inf Div	3rd Parchute Div
	709th Inf Div	5th Parachute Div	
	716th Inf Div	* in the Channel Islands	** Still forming

Where was the main battle to be fought?

While Directive 40 clearly stated that all the defensive actions of the commander must be to defeat the enemy attack before it could reach the coast or, at the latest, on the coast itself, this undoubtedly went against the opinions of many of the advocates of mobile warfare. Rommel was quite clear that the shoreline was the right place to defeat the enemy—witness his dictum: *'Die HKL ist der Strand.'* (The *Hauptkampflinie*—main battle line—is the beach.) His main reason for coming to this conclusion was his personal experience in North Africa of having to move by day under constant enemy air superiority. The casualties both to men and materiel, especially during the Tunisian campaign, had left him with the firm conviction that reserve forces, in particular armour, had to be as far forward as possible, otherwise they would be decimated trying to get into battle. However, his 'fight them on the beaches' policy was not shared by von Rundstedt and other senior officers, who favoured mobile defence.

Behind the tiny chateau of La Roche Guyon rose sheer chalk cliffs into which German engineers blasted a series of tunnels and enlarged some existing old workings, until they had room for living and office quarters for Rommel's 100-plus staff officers and soldiers who manned the HQ. Only senior staff were accommodated in the chateau itself, Rommel occupying a modest ground-floor apartment adjoining the rose garden. By early March all the necessary preparatory work had been done and HQ Army Group B moved in on the evening of 9th. The chateau was owned by the La Rochefoucald family, who were allowed to stay on and with whom everyone on the staff soon formed a pleasant and amicable association. Rommel often shot with the old duke, whilst his younger staff officers flirted with the attractive young daughter of the family.

This became one of the most contentious issues of defence strategy. Panzergruppe West, commanded by General der Panzertruppen Freiherr Geyr von Schweppenburg, who was completely opposed to Rommel's view that reserves had to be forward, brushed aside Rommel's criticisms of his centralised 'out of harm's way' policy by saying that even if the Allied air power affected daylight movement, then the panzers would still be able to move quickly by night. Not only did he fundamentally disagree with Rommel but he also thoroughly disliked the Desert Fox's chief of staff, the General Hans Speidel, commenting on one occasion that Speidel had never commanded anything larger than an infantry company. In a postwar study he reiterated his criticism of Rommel and his theories on panzer movement thus:

'The following Rommel theories were fundamentally unjustified and have been proved to be false:
(a) "Panzer divisions cannot be moved when the enemy has air supremacy." Under skilled leadership 12th SS Panzer Division and 2nd Panzer Division reached their operational area without serious losses. Panzer Lehr Division had its considerable losses only because of Rundstedt's express command to move forward by day, an order foreign to air and armoured warfare.
(b) "A main landing on the Channel Coast is still to be expected." This is a model example of clinging tenaciously to a preconceived opinion.
(c) "Without mobile panzer divisions, landings of fairly great local significance cannot be eliminated." "Pure" panzer divisions cannot fight with their mass and shock effect at all within range of great enemy fleets, least of all in flooded and mined terrain. Anyone who fought in Sicily and Salerno (invasion of Italy) will confirm that. Besides, for the sake of logic it must be stated that it is comparatively easier to bring up panzer divisions from a location far to the rear than to move laterally mobile panzer reserves near the front. If the latter is possible, the first must be too.'

However, the facts are that the movement of 12th SS Panzer Division (Hitlerjugend) and Panzer Lehr to the front was delayed by enemy air attacks and, while they were able to hold the Caen area into July, they were unable to effect the outcome of the invasion. Whether they could have done had they been where Rommel wanted them is conjectural.

Such fundamental points of disagreement were bound to have an effect on the success or failure of the German defence plan, especially when the overall land commander, von Rundstedt, had no direct control over sea and air forces. Clearly the seeds of confusion were there from the outset.

3 FRANCE

The largest country in Western Europe, with long sea coasts, wide beaches and proximity to England, France was the major defensive problem the Germans faced and where the Atlantic Wall was most likely to be attacked.

The Atlantic Coast

On the coast was France's oldest naval base—Brest—heavily protected, as it was now the most important German naval base in France, being ringed by at least 20 coastal batteries and flak positions. Its massive garrison of some 35,000 was under the command of tough paratrooper General der Fallschirmtruppe Hermann-Bernhard Ramcke, who held out until 19 September, and was awarded both the Swords and Diamonds to his Knight's Cross during the siege. The U-boat base at Lorient meant that it, too, was given fortress status, as was St Nazaire. Both were 'sealed off' by the Americans and were left until the end of the war without being assaulted, to keep down the number of unnecessary Allied casualties. Both fortresses were, nevertheless, regularly bombed. Finally, there were the ports/naval bases of La Rochelle, La Pallice, Gironde, Bordeaux and Bayonne facing the Bay of Biscay. La Rochelle, together with the islands of Ré and Oléron, plus the U-boat base at La Pallice, made a formidable fortress with such gunpower as the Karola battery on the Île de Ré, which comprised two of the gun turrets from the unfinished cruiser *Seydlitz*, both mounting two 20.3cm naval guns with a range in excess of 30km. It was also sealed off by American and Free French troops, then subjected to regular bombing raids until mid-April 1945, when it was finally taken.

As the northern Biscay U-boat bases (Brest, St Nazaire, and Lorient) were cut off from inland communications, U-boats from Bordeaux had to assume tasks of supply. At one point U-boats were also carrying ammunition to besieged Cherbourg and St Mâlo. These tasks had to be abandoned with the rapid deterioration of the land situation.

Below: *Ro510 at La Perroche had four 669 casemates fitted with 15.5cm SFH414 (f) guns. Today, this 669 has been well-decorated.* Thierry Llansades

Bottom: *Bordeaux was first used by the Italian Navy as from 1940 the Betasom Flotilla was based there. In 1941 work started on a German bunker that could take 15 boats being 245m wide, 162m long and 19m high. The roof was a substantial 5m thick. U-178 was the first to use the bunker—in January 1943—which would house* 12. Unterseebootsflottille. *U-178 was scuttled in Bordeaux on 25 August 1944.* Thierry Llansades

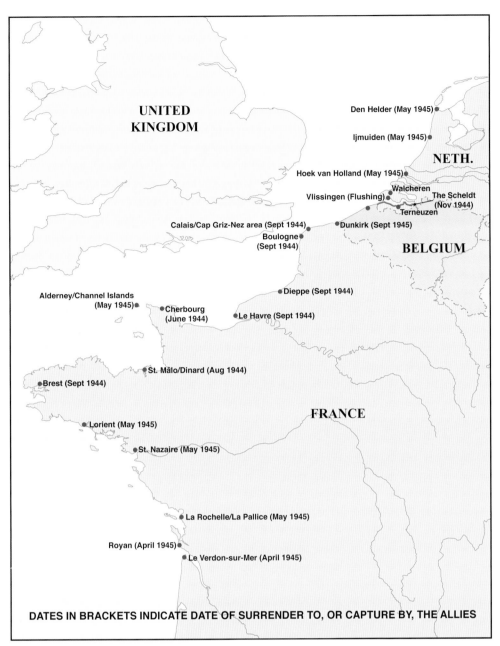

DATES IN BRACKETS INDICATE DATE OF SURRENDER TO, OR CAPTURE BY, THE ALLIES

Map labels:

UNITED KINGDOM

Den Helder (May 1945)

Ijmuiden (May 1945)

NETH.

Hoek van Holland (May 1945)

Walcheren

Vlissingen (Flushing)

The Scheldt (Nov 1944)

Terneuzen

Calais/Cap Griz-Nez area (Sept 1944)

Dunkirk (Sept 1945)

Boulogne (Sept 1944)

BELGIUM

Dieppe (Sept 1944)

Alderney/Channel Islands (May 1945)

Cherbourg (June 1944)

Le Havre (Sept 1944)

St. Mālo/Dinard (Aug 1944)

Brest (Sept 1944)

FRANCE

Lorient (May 1945)

St. Nazaire (May 1945)

La Rochelle/La Pallice (May 1945)

Royan (April 1945)

Le Verdon-sur-Mer (April 1945)

487 Hochleitstand Barbara

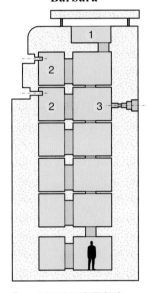

1 COMMUNICATIONS

2 OBSERVATION LEVELS

3 CLOSE DEFENCE

Above: *The famous* Hochleitstand *nicknamed Barbara, part of the Adour-Nord Battery near Bayonne—one of the southernmost of the Atlantic Wall's gun batteries. Initially armed with four old French 165mm, these were replaced in 1944 with more modern German 150mm guns.* Thierry Llansades

Left: *One of the defenses of Brest, a Tobruk with a Somua S35 turret armed with a 4.7cm gun and a 7.5mm Reibel machine gun.* NARA

Fangrost superstructure
Explosion chambers
Triangular void
Pen openings
First layer of reinforced concrete
Second layer of reinforced concrete

The U-Boat Pens

There were five major U-boat bases in France:
- *Bordeaux: 12th Flottilla*
- *Brest: 1st and 9th Flottillas*
- *La Rochelle (La Pallice): 3rd Flottilla*
- *Lorient: 2nd and 10th Flottillas*
- *St Nazaire: 6th and 7th Flottillas*

Construction of these mighty bunkers was handled by Organisation Todt, although the actual work was mainly by French and foreign 'volunteers', to plans created by the Kriegsmarine. Initially this was Amtsgruppe Werft-, Hafen-und Strombau (K IV); after 1 April 1943 it was the newly created Marinebauwesen.
On 24 July 1944 control of all Wehrmacht construction was transferred to Organisation Todt (OT) and Amt Marinebauwesen was redesignated Abteilung Betrieb. The structures were continuously improved, for example by the Fangrost system shown above: inverted, concrete, U-shaped beams set on parallel slabs producing an explosion chamber in the same way spaced armour is used on tanks to defend against RPGs.

Top: *U-203, the first U-Boot to enter the submarine pens at St Nazaire.*

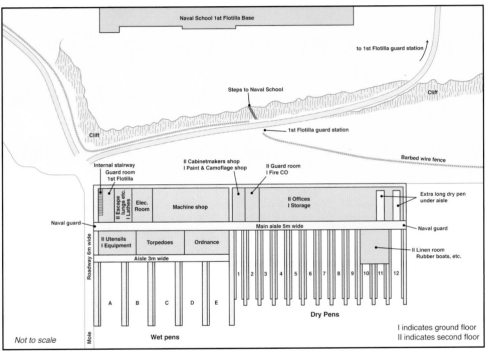

Opposite, Below: *The St Nazaire pens. Building began in February 1941—pens 6, 7 and 8 were completed in June 1941; 9–14 from July 1941 to January 1942; 1–5 in February–June 1942.*

Above and Centre Left: *Construction of the largest of the German sub pens—at Brest in Brittany—started in early 1941. Bombed many times by the Allies, in August 1944 the bunker was hit nine times by Tallboys, five of which penetrated the roof with no damage to the submarines.*

Below Left: *Bombing La Rochelle. The pens at La Pallice are at* **A**. *Bordeaux and La Rochelle (La Pallice) were threatened by the Allies' invasion of southern France on 15 August. By 26 August Bordeaux had become untenable. Dönitz sent: 'The military situation has made it necessary to prepare all U-boats at bases as quickly as possible for combat operation or transfer to Norway.' The following morning the office of FdU West ceased. USAF*

Within the diagram:

Naval School 1st Flotilla Base

to 1st Flotilla guard station

Steps to Naval School

Cliff

Cliff

1st Flotilla guard station

Barbed wire fence

Internal stairway
Guard room
1st Flotilla

II Cabinetmakers shop
I Paint & Camoflage shop

II Guard room
I Fire CO

Extra long dry pen under aisle

Naval guard

II Escape lungs etc. I Lathes

Elec. Room

Machine shop

II Offices I Storage

Naval guard

Main aisle 5m wide

II Utensils I Equipment

Torpedoes

Ordnance

II Linen room Rubber boats, etc.

Aisle 3m wide

Roadway 6m wide

A   B   C   D   E

1 2 3 4 5 6 7 8 9 10 11 12

Dry Pens

Not to scale

Mole

Wet pens

I indicates ground floor
II indicates second floor

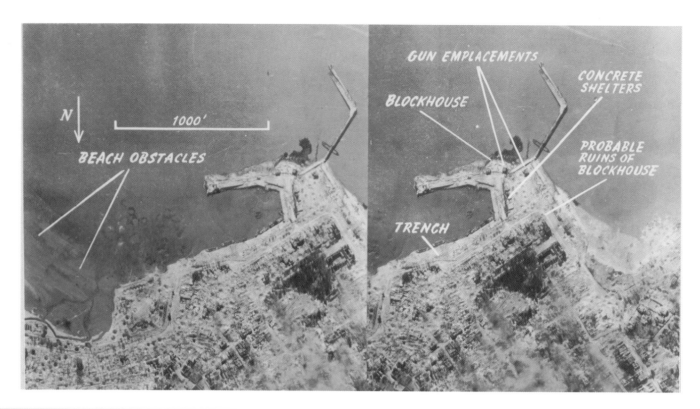

The labels on the image read:
- N
- 1000'
- BEACH OBSTACLES
- GUN EMPLACEMENTS
- BLOCKHOUSE
- CONCRETE SHELTERS
- PROBABLE RUINS OF BLOCKHOUSE
- TRENCH

The Atlantic Coast

Above and Left: *Two fortresses defended the Gironde Estuary: north, at Royan (4) and south, at La Pointe de Grave (5). Royan was attacked in the early hours of 5 January 1945 and obliterated, although the harbour is still identifiable today. USAF (Above)*

Below Left: *This 637 fire measurement position is part of the HKB Hamburg, itself part of Festung Girond-Nord. Today it is one of a number of bunkers in the surf just north of St Palais-sur-Mer (4). JLPC/Wikimedia Commons/CC-BY-SA-3.0*

Opposite:
Above Left: *The islands off the Atlantic coast were well defended. Here the chateau d'Oléron is bombed. USAF*

Above Right: *Ars en Ré (1) off La Rochelle was the site of HKB Kora (Ro425) and MKB Karola (Ro429) batteries constructed 1942–44: Kora had four 22cm guns in open ring positions; Karola 20.3cm guns from the cruiser Seydlitz. The seven-storey S497 Leitstand for Karola is a 25m-tall beauty. There was an MFlak battery (Ro424 Kathe) nearby. Thierry Llansades*

Center Right: *M272 casemate for a 15cm gun, part of MKB Hertha (2), Ro417, on the Île de Ré. Thierry Llansades*

Right: *With the Sablanceaux bridge arcing towards the Île de Ré in the background, the foreground is dominated by the 120a artillery observation post with armoured turret. It's part of Ro227 Damian, a Flak position defending the airfield (3). Thierry Llansades*

Right: *The U-boat base at Saint Nazaire is at **A**. It was unaffected by Operation 'Chariot' in March 1942 that saw the HMS Campbeltown, packed full of explosives, used to destroy the Normandie dock, thereby eliminating St Nazaire as a repair facility for Tirpitz.* USAF

Below Right: *One of the most impressive sights on the Atlantic coast is the S414 fire control stand at Batz-sur-Mer—one of only a few such bunkers still to be seen. The S414 was linked to 4./MAA280, two 24cm railway guns, and was camouflaged as a hotel.* JLPC/Wikimedia Commons/CC-BY-SA-3.0

Below, Inset: *The defences of St Mâlo stretched to Dinard, a nearby resort whose beaches were studded with the usual* Hemmelbalker *and mined stakes.* USAF (L)

Below: *The battery at Tréogat was one of three west of Quimper on the Finisterre coast. The four 669 bunkers housed 76.2mm PaK 39(r) weapons.* 25asd/WikiCommons

Opposite, Above Left and Right, and Centre: *The St Mâlo citadel fell to the US Army on 17 August, although the Island of Cezembre held out till 2 September.* NARA

Opposite, Below: *An FT17 turret on a Tobruk at pointe de Bloscan, Roscoff.* NARA

Brittany

Home to the important naval bases at Lorient, St Nazaire and Brest, the Atlantic Wall in Brittany was not just there to defend against an invasion but to protect the only truly strategic weapon the Third Reich possessed: the *U-Boot-Waffe*. Without a strategic bombing capability, the undersea arm was the main way that Germany projected its power into the Atlantic and sustained an all-out attack on Britain's merchant shipping, with the U-boat as the primary weapon. This led to significant defensive work on the submarine pens and their bases which had been designated by Hitler as fortresses "to be defended to the last man, to the last cartridge". Much of the Allied strategic bombing campaign had been directed at the *U-Boot-Waffe* and, as part of the breakout from the Normandy beachhead, the US Army spent some weeks between August and October 1944 subduing the peninsula of Brittany hoping to secure a major port to help the Allies' supply problems, and to negate the U-boat threat. The Americans swept through the peninsula finding fewer troops than expected: most of them were in the fortresses. 6th Armored reached Brest on 6 August: it took five weeks to take the city defended by General der Fallschirmtruppe Hermann-Bernhard Ramcke and 40,000 men. Ramcke surrendered on 19 September, a month after St Mâlo, under the command of General Andreas von Aulock, had fallen. Ringed by defences and with a garrison of some 12,000, St Mâlo's Citadel and the Isle of Cezembre held out longest, even after napalm attacks and shelling by British battleships

Rather than sustain further heavy casualties—10,000 at Brest—the Allies decided to bypass the other two Breton ports—Lorient and St Nazaire—and did the same for La Rochelle further south. With their supply lines cut and access by sea interdicted, their garrisons were bottled up and could do nothing to affect the outcome of the war. Lorient, the most important of the bases, was where Grossadmiral Karl Dönitz, commander of the *U-Boot-Waffe*, had set up his HQ. The three huge Keroman submarine pens were not affected seriously by the bombing that destroyed 90 percent of the surrounding city. General Fahrmbacher finally surrendered the city on 10 May 1945, and General Junck, commander of the St Nazaire garrison followed suit the next day.

Guernsey Batteries

Navy
1 Mirus 4 x 305mm K14 (r)
2 Strassburg 4 x 220mm K532 (f)
3 Steinbruch 4 x 150mm SK C/28

Army
4 Dollmann 4 x 220mm K532 (f)
5 Radetzsky 4 x 220mm K532 (f)
6 Elefant 3 x 210mm Mrs 18
7 Mammut 3 x 210mm Mrs 18
8 Rhinozeros 3 x 210mm Mrs 18
9 Gneisenau 4 x 150mm K18 (transferred to Jersey August 1944)
10 Scharnhorst 4 x 150mm K18 (transferred to Jersey August 1944)
11 Barbara 4 x 155mm K418 (f)
12 Naumannshöhe 4 x 105mm K331 (f)

Div
13 Georgsfeste
14 Sperber 4 x 100mm lFH 14/19 (t)
15 Tiger 4 x 100mm lFH 14/19 (t)
16 Wolf 4 x 100mm lFH 14/19 (t)
17 Lux 4 x 100mm lFH 14/19 (t)

Channel Islands

Nowhere on the Atlantic Wall was there a greater concentration of German forces on the ground than in the Channel Islands, where 319th Infantry Division—the strongest division in the entire Heer—was located, together with numerous Kriegsmarine personnel manning the naval batteries, and Luftwaffe personnel manning anti-aircraft guns. By way of example, here is the personnel strength on the three main islands just three months after D-Day, when the islands still expected to be invaded at any moment:

BRANCH OF SERVICE	GUERNSEY	JERSEY	ALDERNEY	TOTAL
Army—Infantry	4,150	3,900	800	8,850
Anti-tank	430	360	-	790
Tank	180	130	20	330
Artillery	520	820	70	1,410
Coast artillery	1,130	1,120	150	2,400
Engineers	90	360	10	460
Signals	180	120	70	370
Supply	720	1,150	200	2,070
Air Force	1,850	1,450	1,050	4,350
Navy	1,420	1,890	150	3,460
Construction Troops	310	150	150	610
Total	10,980	11,450	2,670	25,100

There were five large coastal batteries on Alderney, 15 on Guernsey and eight on Jersey. The largest was Batterie Mirus comprising four 30.5cm guns on Guernsey, the guns being from the Imperial Russian Navy battleship *Imperator Alexandr III*. In addition to the coastal batteries and their impressive observation towers, there were many smaller fortifications. Much of the work was done by slave labour and there were four concentration camps in Alderney. However, the defences were not tested by invasion as the Allies bypassed the islands to reduce casualties.

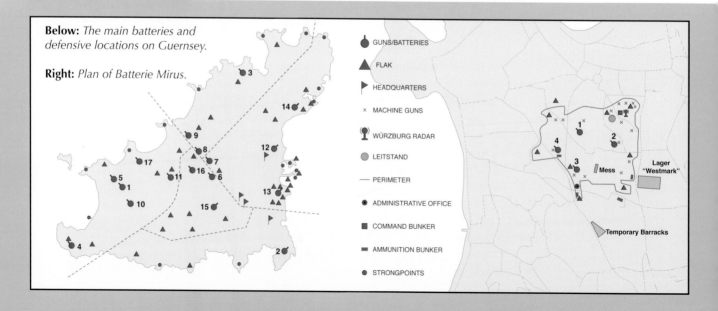

Below: *The main batteries and defensive locations on Guernsey.*

Right: *Plan of Batterie Mirus.*

GUNS/BATTERIES

FLAK

HEADQUARTERS

MACHINE GUNS

WÜRZBURG RADAR

LEITSTAND

PERIMETER

ADMINISTRATIVE OFFICE

COMMAND BUNKER

AMMUNITION BUNKER

STRONGPOINTS

Lager "Westmark"

Mess

Temporary Barracks

Above: *Important Atlantic Wall locations on Guernsey.*
1 *Fort Hommet 105mm coastal defence gun casement bunker entrance.*
2 *Fort Hommet (StP Rotenstein).*
3 *Marine Peilstelle 2 on L'Erée headland (StP Langenberg). Next to it a shelter for a 150cm Mirus searchlight.*
4 *The largest guns to be emplaced on the Channel Islands, Batterie Mirus boasted four 30.5cm guns from the* Imperator Aleksandr III, *renamed General Alexeiev.*
5 *Heer observation stand M5.*
6 *Naval direction and rangefinding tower MP4. Built on five levels, each was to have served an MKB but as there were only three, the two other levels were used by the Heer. A Freya radar was mounted on the roof.*

Left: *An 670 facing the northern part of Grouville Bay, Jersey.* Paweł 'pbm' Szubert/WikiCommons/ CC-BY-SA-3.0

Centre Left: *The 631 on St Ouen's Bay at La Carrière enfilades the beach in front of the* Panzermauer.

Below Left: *At* **A** *the unique seven-inch thick armoured cupolas of the M132 Leitstand for MKB Lothringen manned by the 3./MAA604. Visible at* **B** *the top (and entrance) of MP1 which has a 2cm Flak emplacement on it.* WikiCommons

Normandy and Upper Normany

Opposite:
Above Right: *Fort du Roule—StP255—overlooked Cherbourg with an MKB of four 671 gun emplacements at* **1, 2, 4, 5**. *They were armed with 105mm SK C/32.U U-Boot guns. At* **3**, *the SK Leitstand.* NARA

Centre Left and Right: *Then and now views of Cherbourg's Gare Maritime. Today only two bunkers remain, a 631 (***A***) for 4.7cm ATk gun and a 649 casemate with a 2cm Flak on top (***B***), visible in front of French nuclear submarine Le Redoutable, which is part of the Cité de la Mer museum.* NARA

Below Left: *Map showing the defences of Cherbourg as the US Army attacked.* CMH

Below Right: *The pier at Querqueville. At left WN220 Fort Chavagnac.* NARA

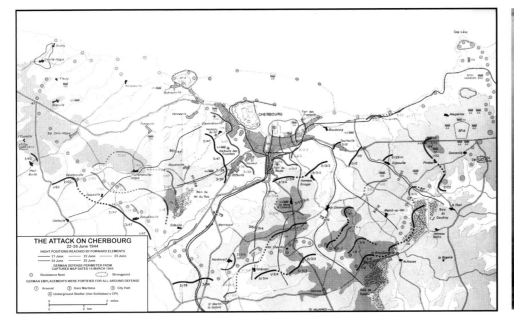

THE ATTACK ON CHERBOURG
22–26 June 1944

NIGHT POSITIONS REACHED BY FORWARD ELEMENTS
- 21 June
- 22 June
- 23 June
- 24 June
- 25 June

GERMAN DEFENSE PERIMETER FROM
CAPTURED MAP DATED 14 MARCH 1944

Resistance Nest   Strongpoint

GERMAN EMPLACEMENTS WERE FORTIFIED FOR ALL-AROUND DEFENSE

① Arsenal   ② Gare Maritime   ③ City Hall
④ Underground Shelter (Von Schlieben's CP)

0   2 miles
0   2 km

3 and 4 *155mm gun in a casemate at HKB Gatteville, as abandoned in June 1944 by 7./HKAR1261 when the position was taken by 24th Cavalry Recon Sqn who had been tasked with protecting 4th Inf Div's right flank as they attacked Cherbourg. NARA*

5 *The impressive SK Leitstand for the Batterie Seeadler which looks out to sea between Le Brick and Fermanville, east of Cherbourg.*

There had been much debate about where the Allies would eventually strike, and while the Pas de Calais was at the forefront, Normandy's golden beaches were also an obvious choice. The Atlantic Wall in this area—from the Cotentin peninsula and Festung Cherbourg through Le Havre to Tréport—has obviously been extremely well covered in many books. This was the area that saw the invasion and much of the fighting in summer 1944 and there is a wealth of published material and visible evidence on the ground, albeit much-damaged from the fighting. Because of this, our whistle-stop tour of the Atlantic Wall is necessarily brief, with material that gives a flavour of the area rather than a detailed tour.

Cherbourg (see p67) at the top of the Cotentin peninsula was a designated fortress, protected by a considerable number of heavy batteries and strongpoints from Framville to Gerville-Hague. It would take the Americans heavy fighting until 27 June before the port was captured, only for them to find that the port's facilities had been so completely destroyed that it could not be used for some time. The Cotentin peninsula itself was crowded with gun batteries, coastal defences and flooded areas to restrict enemy movements. However, the coastal defences were at their strongest opposite Omaha Beach, which had been identified as a strong candidate for invasion. The coast from the River Vire to the River Orne was well-defended with plenty of batteries, although the Atlantic Wall was unfinished in the area. There was much building in process and the area would have been even more difficult to attack if the Allies had procrastinated for any length of time.

Upper Normandy, from Le Havre to Tréport and the boundary with the Channel Coast, was also well protected, in some areas such as from Dieppe to Le Havre, by the cliffs which formed a natural barrier. Dieppe did not receive fortress status (indeed, it was surrendered without a fight to the Canadians in September 1944) but Festung Le Havre which protected the mouth of the River Seine was one of the best-defended of the fortresses on the Atlantic Wall, with a total of 15 gun batteries (eight Kriegsmarine, four Heer and three Luftwaffe Flak) with battery positions, radar bunkers, beach defences, fire control towers and so on, from Fécamp north of Le Havre down to Deauville and Riva Bella on the coast northwest of Caen. One of the heaviest batteries defending Le Havre was the 38cm naval gun at Le Grand Hameau, which had a range of some 22 miles, covering the mouth of the Orne river.

The area was also studded with V-1 and V-2 installations, including assembly plants and launching sites, important targets for the Allies to relieve the pressure on the civilian population.

1 and 2 *MKB Hamburg's No 1 Turm (**Left**) which was put out of action by gunfire during a duel with SS* Texas. *The battery, StP234, was armed with four 24cm guns. NARA*

6 *Three of the 679s housing the 155mm K420 (f) mle16 guns of HKB Gatteville, StP152. Behind them (**7**) are the open emplacements used before the casemates were built.*

8 *The Luftwaffe Radar Station Tausendfüssler, StP235, is located at Carneville Osteck above Batterie Seeadler. It was equipped with a number of radars.*

Opposite:
1, 2, 3, 4 *Barfleur was the port that saw William The Conqueror leave for England in 1066. In 1944 it was protected by WN121 Le Cracko with an anti-tank wall on the harbour and a number of bunkers—including a position for a 5cm KwK now under the lighthouse at the southern breakwater (**A**). At **B and 3** a 677 allowed an 88mm PaK 41/43 to face La Sambière beach. The Tobruk (**3**) gives a good view of the field of fire (**C and 2**).*

5 *Further down the coast, StP111 St Vaast, had a 667 bunker for 50mm KwK protecting the harbour entrance and a large SK bunker that used the Fishermen's church as protection from bombardment.*
6 *Two Vf MG posts on the breakwater.*
7 *Tobruk at the base of the breakwater looking toward La Houge.*
8 *Vf MG post, part of StP110 La Hougue.*
9 *Aerial view of St Vaast La Hougue.*

Above Left: *StP142 HKB Crasville was a battery of four casemates—two 650s and two 671s, as here—for 105mm K331(f) guns.* NARA

Centre Left: *A wonderful observation position looking towards St Vaast, La Pernelle—WN144—was a Type 120a with an armoured cupola as here and a Vf6a observation bunker.*

Below Left: *Point de Landemer La Houe, WN119—an emplacement for a 5cm KwK on the beach looking toward Barfleur, just around the point from St Vaast.*

Part of the Atlantic Wall   Sept. 21, 1944
6 men from L Co. hurt here   Quineville
6 killed

1

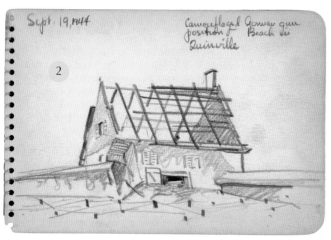

Sept. 19, 1944   Camouflaged German gun
position & Beach in
Quinville

2

Beach & barbed wire entanglement at
Quinville   Sept. 19, 1944

3

Beach & barbed wire
6 killed

4

5

6

7

72

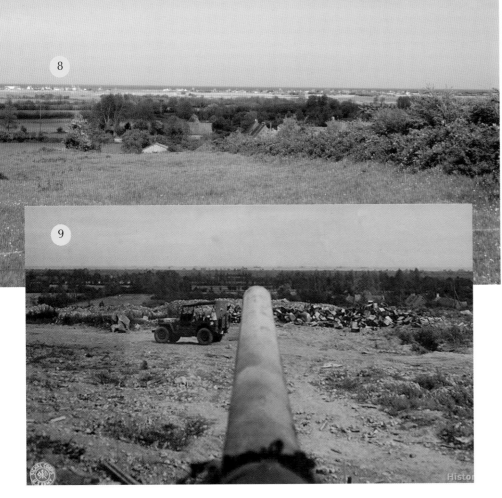

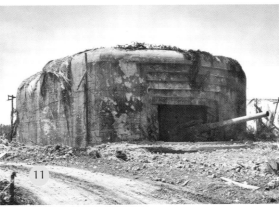

1, 2, 3 *Victor A. Lundy, who served in the US 26th Inf Div, sketched scenes of his army life from training through to November 1944 when he was wounded. These three sketches show the Atlantic Wall at Quinéville around 19 September. Quinéville was a key component of the German defence, anchoring the backstop line for the forward defensive positions north of Utah Beach. It was taken after a stern battle on 14 June. The sketches were captioned thus by Lundy:* **1** *'Part of the Atlantic Wall, Quinéville 6 men from L Co. hurt here, 6 killed';* **2** *'Camouflaged German gun position, beach in Quinéville';* **3** *'Beach & barbed wire entanglement at Quinéville'. Note in particular the barbed wire and anti-tank walls: today, most of what is left of the defences tends to be the large structures built of reinforced concrete and one forgets just how many other layers of defences there were: trenches, roadblocks, flooded areas, anti-tank positions—all highly camouflaged and a problem for the attackers.* Library of Congress

4, 5, 6, 7: *Batterie Azeville, StP133, had four 650 casemates armed with 10.5cm Schneider K331(f) guns and manned by 2./HAAR1261. The fire control position was at Batterie Crisbecq/ St Marcouf.* NARA

8, 9, 10, 11: *StP134 Batterie Crisbecq had four 21cm K39/41 guns, two housed in 683 bunkers as here. Their field of fire was restricted in the bunkers which were also targets for air strikes, but their position on higher ground gave them raking fields of fire over the coast.* NARA (9,11)

Utah Beach was at the limit of the range of the batteries at Azeville and Crisbecq but they did some damage to naval forces, including sinking a destroyer, and they proved a hard nut to crack. Even when Azeville was overrun, fire from Crisbecq was called down to clear the American attackers. US 22nd Inf finally took Azeville on 9 June; Crisbecq was abandoned on the night of 11/12 June, the battery personnel retreating to Cherbourg.

Right: The flat expanse of Utah Beach. Note the 5cm KwK gun position. NARA

Below Right: The casualties were lighter at Utah than Omaha but the fighting intensified as the US Army fought first to cut off the Cotentin Peninsula and then to take Cherbourg. NARA

Below: The terrain around Utah Beach is low-lying and much of it was easily flooded by the Germans.

Opposite: Utah Beach today, the circular building is the museum. The plan shows WN5 (**Inset**), the strongpoint that defended what became the main exit from the beach. Today's museum sits on the site of a Tobruk with a 37mm-armed Renault tank turret, which has been incorporated into the museum. Further down the beach there is a monument (**A**) to the engineers who cleared the beach of obstacles on D-Day. It is mounted on top of a Type 702 bunker, one of five in this area. The largest guns were 50mm and 47mm, the former housed in Type 667 casemates. The area behind the coastline was flooded to the west and surrounded by barbed wire and minefields, forcing the attackers to use the narrow roads that led off the beach inland.

FIRE TRENCHES

BARBED WIRE

MINEFIELD

FORTIFICATIONS

Châlet Rouge

High Water

MG

Bunker H 702

50mm KWK gun position

Bunker H 501

H 702

Ammunition store H 134

Step Mont

Bunker H 702

4.7cm Pak

to Ste. Marie-du-Mont

Tobruk H 69

H 702

MG

MG

Tobruk H 69

Tobruk H 67 for a 37mm tank turret

Tobruk H 206 (50mm)

Casemate H 667 for 50mm gun

H 134

50mm KWK gun position

A

Top and Above Left and Left: *Grandcamp Maisy is a bustling seaside resort to the west of Pointe du Hoc. Double 5cm KwK position, this is part of WN82. On its right is the back end of a Tobruk. Nearby are Tobruks for mortar and tank turret. NARA*

Above: *Aerial view of Grandcamp-Maisy showing: (**1**) Pointe du Hoc; (**2**) WN81 Grandcamp West 667 and tank turret Tobruk; (**3**) WN81 double KwK bunker (two openings with traversable gun; (**4**) Grandcamp Maisy batteries—see below— off photo in this direction; (**5**) WN82.*

Below Left: *There were two artillery batteries at Grandcamp Maisy: WN83 had six 15.5cm sFH 414(f) guns manned by 9./AR1716; the other four 10cm 14/19 Skoda (t) light howitzers manned by 8./AR1716. The guns were heavily bombed on the night of 5/6 June but this didn't stop the battery opening fire on D-Day; a naval bombardment followed but did not silence them. On the morning of 9 June the defenders of this large complex of trenches and bunkers were attacked by 2nd and 5th Rangers, soldiers from the 116th Inf Regt (29th Div), and 81st Chemical Weapons Bn (mortars). It was eventually captured by the 5th Rangers.*

Opposite: *At the western end of Omaha Beach, the Pointe du Hoc Battery seemed a potent threat. It was attacked early on 6 June by the US Ranger Assault Group under the command of Lt-Col James E. Rudder. The plan (**Right**) called for the cliffs to be scaled. The unit sustained significant casualties in its daring attack, but took the position and held it until relieved on D+2 in spite of counterattacks from the German 916th Grenadier Regt. The guns, however, were not there. The Germans had moved them inland while casemates were constructed. NARA*

Opposite, Below Left: *This regiment, AR1716, played a critical role in the D-Day battles with units ranged along the Normandy beaches.*

Artillerie-Regiment 1716
CO: Oberstleutnant Helmut Knüppe

I./AR1716 (Gefechtsstand: Colomby)
1. Bty Merville: four 10cm leFH14/19(t)
2. Bty WN16 (Colleville-sur-Orne) four 10cm leFH14/19(t)
3. Bty Bréville (northeast of Caen) four 7.5cm FK16 nA
4. Bty WN12 (Ouistreham "Water Tower Battery") four 15cm sFH414(f)
10. Bty (4km NE of Bayeux "Graf Waldersee Batterie") three 15cm sFH13 auf Lorraine-Schlepper

II./AR1716 (Gefechtsstand: Crépon)
5. Bty WN35b (Crépon) four 10cm leFH14/19(t)
6. Bty WN32 (la Mare-Fontaine) four 10cm leFH14/19(t)
7. Bty WN28a (Bény-sur-Mer) four 10cm leFH14/19(t)

III./AR1716 (attached to 352. Inf Div -10. Bty)*
Gefechtsstand: Le Cambe
8. Bty WN84 (Maisy La Martinière) four 10cm leFH14/19(t)
9. Bty WN83 (Maisy Les Perruques) four 15cm sFH414(f)

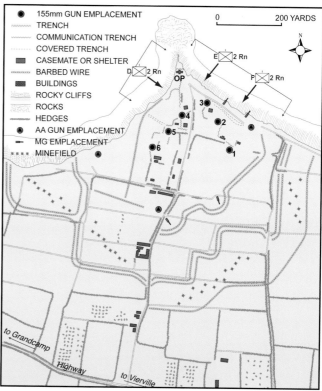

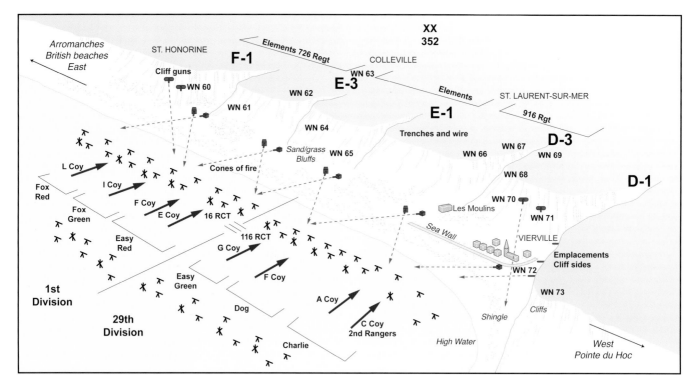

Arromanches
British beaches
East

ST. HONORINE

F-1

Cliff guns

WN 60

WN 61

Elements 726 Regt

WN 63

E-3

WN 62

WN 64

XX
352

COLLEVILLE

Elements

ST. LAURENT-SUR-MER

E-1

916 Rgt

Trenches and wire

D-3

WN 67

WN 66

WN 69

WN 65

Sand/grass
Bluffs

Cones of fire

L Coy

Fox
Red

I Coy

Fox
Green

F Coy

E Coy

16 RCT

Easy
Red

116 RCT

WN 68

WN 70

Les Moulins

WN 71

VIERVILLE

Sea Wall

D-1

Emplacements
Cliff sides

1st
Division

29th
Division

G Coy

F Coy

Easy
Green

Dog

A Coy

C Coy
2nd Rangers

WN 72

WN 73

Shingle

Cliffs

High Water

West
Pointe du Hoc

Charlie

1

2

Top: *Omaha Beach was the best-defended of all the invasion beaches. Steve Zaloga's excellent* The Devil's Garden *analyses the defences carefully and shows there were more defensive MGs and ATk weapons, heavier artillery support, and a more defendable position than elsewhere. The US forces also lacked tank support—the DD tanks were launched too far out—and had no specialised equipment such as the British 79th Armoured Division 'Funnies'. Nevertheless, in spite of heavy casualties, the beach was taken and held. The Atlantic Wall's best-defended Normandy sector had not been able to hold back the Allies.*

1 *This 677 bunker housing an 88mm PaK 43/41, part of WN61 at Colleville-sur-Mer, became an aid post after the battle. NARA*

2 *WN66 protected Les Moulins D-3 draw. NARA*

3 *The field of fire from the bluffs is well illustrated in this photo of trenches overlooking Easy Red Beach west of E-1 draw. NARA*

4 *The rear of the 667 casemate housing a 5cm KwK that proved such an effective element of WN65 covering the E-1 St Laurent draw. NARA*

3

4

The flat golden sands of Omaha Beach look wonderful today. These are the key locations:

1 WN60 at the east end of the beach had the reverse panorama to the main photo, looking west to Vierville.

2 E-3 draw led up to Colleville. Highlighted are **A** WN61 on east side of draw; **B** The Big Red One memorial on top of WN62, the most effective defensive position on Omaha; **C** WN62 included two 669 casemates; **D** the US cemetery at Colleville.

3 E-1 draw today. The bunker at **4** opposite is identified at **E**.

4 Vierville, the most heavily defended part of the beach. WN70–73 had four ATk casemates, ten MG bunkers or Tobruks, and four mortar Tobruks—creating a killing zone that decimated the first wave of the 116th RCT. Various significant memorials can be found here, particularly that of the National Guard (**F**).

Ⓐ

Left and Inset: *The battery at Longues—WN48—is an impressive reminder of the strength of the Atlantic Wall. Completed in 1944, it was built and manned by the Kriegsmarine although under Heer control. The four 152mm guns, housed in M272 casemates, posed a significant threat to the Allies, and so it was bombed heavily and on the 6th it was bombarded by the French cruiser* Georges Leygues *and USS* Arkansas. *This didn't stop the battery itself firing 170 shots before it was effectively silenced by British cruisers* Ajax *and* Argonaut. *It surrendered to the British 231st Inf Bde on the 7th.*

Centre and Below Left: *Port-en-Bessin was captured by 47 RM Cdo in a great feat of arms. The unit landed 12 miles away on Gold Beach, infiltrated enemy lines, and made their way to the port. On the evening of 7 June when darkness fell, Capt Terence Cousins, who died in the attack, led 25 men up the hill and charged the enemy bunkers past the Vauban Tower at* **A** *and took the garrison prisoner.*

Above Right and Inset:
Arromanches today.
A *Place du 6 Juin, the point where the centre roadway of Mulberry B, constructed by Nos 969 and 970 Port Floating Equipment Coys, reached land. The Mulberry harbour concept was something the Germans did not expect and ensured they focused on the Allies' need for a port, defending Cherbourg and Le Havre in more depth than the coast.*

B *A number of roadway-supporting 'Beetles' still can be seen on the beach.*

C *One of two 612 casemates that defended Arromanches. On this one sits M4A2 Sherman* Berry au Bac *of Gen Leclerc's 2nd Armored Division.*

Right: *Further west along Gold Beach is A37 Asnelles. At* **D** *an 669 armed with an 88mm did a lot of damage to the British landings. Sextons of 511 Battery knocked out this casemate over open sights. At* **E** *a casemate for a 5cm KwK PaK L/60 gun.*

A Canadians study a sand model of the Courseulles-sur-Mer area.

B Aerial view of WN31 Courseulles defended by a 75mm gun, two 50mm guns, six machine guns and two 5cm mortars, manned by soldiers of 6./ IR736. The beach was assaulted by B and D Company of The Royal Winnipeg Rifles, with support from A Squadron of the 6th Canadian Armd Regt (1st Hussars). A powerful strongpoint, the Canadians had to battle hard to beat a determined foe. Photo shows:

1 KwK stand.
2 630 casemate.
3 612 casemate near the gigantic Cross of Lorraine memorial to General de Gaulle who arrived on 14 June.
4 The Canadian Juno Beach Centre.

C, D and E Douvres-la-Délivrande—StP Distelfink—is one of the few German radar installations to survive the war. Today a museum, it was completed in autumn 1943 designed to sound the alert when bombers reached German airspace. A number of radars were installed: a Siemens Wasserman, two Freya, and two Würzburg Riese and the location was fortified with bunkers for the 230 personnel. Tobruks including one with a tank turret, anti-tank 5cm KwK stands, Flak emplacements and minefields. Indeed, so well defended was it that it took an attack by 41 Cdo supported by artillery bombardment, flails and ARVEs of 79th Armd Div to take it on 17 June. Note the KwK (**Opposite, Top Right**) stand and the Würzburg radar antenna visible in both photos on this page.

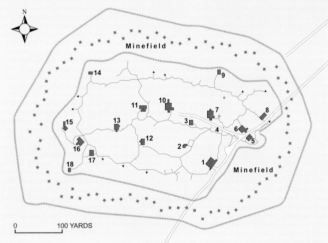

Above and Left: *1st Suffolks was tasked with taking three strongpoints on the outskirts of Colleville (now Colleville-Montgomery): WN16, codenamed 'Morris', a battery of four 100mm guns in three 669 bunkers; then 'Daimler' just to the south; and finally, the strongest: WN18 'Hillman', HQ 736th Grenadier Regt, with a number of bunkers and MG Tobruks, linked by trenches, surrounded by minefields and barbed wire (see key below). After an initial attack failed, a second assault supported by 13th/18th Hussars' Shermans carried the position. The Germans surrendered, but the Hussars lost two tanks and the Suffolks lost seven dead with 24 wounded. The hero was Pte J.R. 'Bunker' Hunter who won a DCM for bravery by single-handedly knocking out the metal cupola of the command bunker.*

Above Left: *Plan of 'Hillman' showing: 1 Memorial above 605 shelter for two guns (and* **Left***); 2 Well; 3 Cistern; 4 Road bridge over trench; 5 Guard post; 6 Kitchens; 7 Command Post A (608) with additional armoured cupola (the one now there isn't the original); 8 Guard post beside road; 9 14/18 58c Tobruks; 0 Command Post B (608); 19 Encircling barbed wire and minefield; 20 Trench system; 11–17 other underground bunkers not part of museum.*

Left and Below: *Ouistreham today is known as a ferry port. This photo shows a number of Atlantic Wall locations around the mouth of the Orne.* **1** *Franceville StP05 defended the eastern flank of the entrance to the port. The site included a 1779 fort, which had two tank turrets, and various fire control posts, crew quarters and bunkers, including an 612 enfilading the estuary and* **2** *Merville Battery (see p. 86).* **3** *WN07 defended the entrance to Ouistreham port.* **4** *Today a museum, the 52-feet-high 'Grand Bunker Musée Le Mur d'Atlantique', was designed as a Flak tower to control the AA defense of the harbour and was in control of the batteries covering the port.* **5** *The Kieffer Flame— commemorating Philippe Kieffer's 1st BFM Commando—erected in 1984 on top of a WN10 Sechsschartenturm turret.*

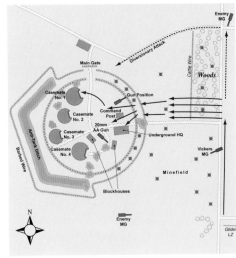

CASEMATES COMPLETED

CASEMATES UNDER CONSTRUCTION

This Page: *Manned by 1./1716, the Merville Battery guns were 10cm leFH14/19 (t) in four casemates—a 611, a 669 and two 612s. Taken by assault by around 150 men of the 9th Parachute Bn led by Lt Terence Otway (whose bust is in the photo* **Above**)*—rather fewer than the 750 sent to do the job. The survivors—some 75–80 men—were unable to destroy the guns as they had no explosives. They did what they could and then moved on to attack Le Plain. The battery was retaken by the Germans and held out until August, but was unable to fire effectively on the British beaches. The battery museum today includes a C-47 Dakota of US Ninth Air Force that took part in the Normandy landings.*

Above, Above Right and Right: *Le Havre, at the mouth of the River Seine, has always been an important port—the second largest in France, after Marseille. It was almost completely destroyed by the war, being bombed over 130 times by the Allies—the worst on 5 and 6 September 1944 when the RAF attacked the city centre and the port. The Nazis destroyed the port infrastructure and sank ships before leaving the city. There were over 5,000 civilian deaths (including 1,770 in 1944), and 75,000–80,000 injured. The defences of Le Havre were considerable, right from the harbour entrance. This is the north pier with a gun casemate, a Flak position as well as a searchlight position; the south pier had more Flak positions. The fighting stopped on 12 September 1944 and the work of rebuilding started.*

Below: *The blockhouse on rue de Trigauville in Le Havre was an SK building for the hospital.* Philippe Alès/WikiCommons/ CC BY-SA 3.0

Left: *Fécamp was an important location between Le Havre and Dieppe, with a number of installations. Perhaps most interesting is the huge bunker on Cap Fagnet (**Above**) that was due to receive a Mammut long-range, phased array, early warning radar. Also on the eastern cliffs was StP09 Notre Dame du Salut, two 612 casemates housing 75mm guns. On the northern slope above the town are a sequence of bunkers, the two visible here are a 630 above a 676 (**Centre**). In the town itself were two Skoda 47mm guns and another 630. Further east was Fe01 Ferme de la Pastourelle, a large complex with a number of bunkers including a 680, 677, four 621s and four 634s with six-embrasured turrets. There is also a 636 (**Below**) controlling a battery of six 155mm captured French guns. Also in the town is a military hospital dug into the chalk cliffs. Daniel*D/ WikiCommons*

Above Left and Right: *Tunnels in the cliffs outside Dieppe (**Left**) and Ault east of Le Tréport (**Right**). So-called 'Dicing' missions by low-flying PR aircraft supplied planners with detailed information about Atlantic Wall emplacements and defences. NARA*

Below, Left and Right: *Dieppe has a special place in the history of the Atlantic Wall thanks to the disastrous raid of 19 August 1942 that saw 3,367 Canadians killed, wounded, or taken prisoner. The events made Churchill determined to be cautious about repeating the cross-Channel attack, gave the Germans a view on what they should expect, convincing them that the Allies would strike at a port. Canadian 2nd Inf Div returned to Dieppe and liberated the city on 1 September 1944, but Operation 'Fusilade', the planned set-piece assault, proved unnecessary as the Germans withdrew. USAF*

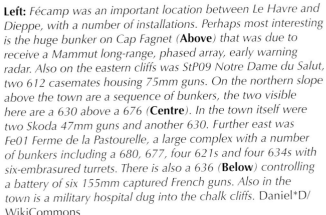

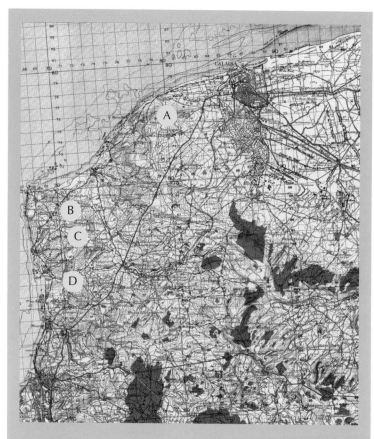

This map shows the German coastal guns in the Calais–Boulogne area in particular the four heavy batteries in the Pas de Calais at **A**. Sangatte, **B**. Framzelle, **C**. Haringzelle and **D**. La Treserorie. From east to west:

204 Naval Coast Bn
- Malo Terminus (4x 194mm)
- HQ-Ostend, St Pol-sur-Mer (3x 145mm)

244 Naval Coast Bn
- Walden Battery (4×170mm)
- Oldenburg Battery (2x 240mm)
- Calais-Dique Est battery (3x 75mm)
- Calais-Bastion II battery (3x 194mm)
- Calais-Fort Lapin battery (2x 164mm)
- Sangatte battery (3x 170mm)
- **Lindemann (A)** Sangatte battery (3x 406mm)

242 Naval Coast Bn
- Wissant-M3 battery (4x 150mm)
- **Grosser Kurfürst (B)** Framzelle battery (4x 280mm)
- Cap Gris-Nez battery with (3x 170mm)
- **Todt (C)** Haringzelle battery with (4x 380mm)

240 Naval Coast Bn
- **Friedrich August (D)** Wimille-Le Tresorerie battery (3x 305mm)
- Boulogne-Fort de la Creche Ouest battery (4x 75mm)
- Boulogne-Fort de la Creche battery (2x 240mm, 1x 194mm, and 4x 105mm)
- Boulogne-Cap d'Alprech battery (4x 94mm)
- Boulogne-Mont de Couppe battery (1x 150mm and 3x 138mm)
- Boulogne-Breakwater battery (4x 88mm)

Railway batteries
- Calais Grables 690 Railway battery (2x 280mm)
- Sangatte-Cement Factory battery (2x 280mm)
- Les Alleux battery (280mm)
- Hydrequent-Le Carre de Marbee battery (1x 280mm)
- Wimereux-Les Oies battery (2x 280mm)

The Channel Coast

In northern France, the fortresses of Dunkerque, Calais, Boulogne and Le Havre were all well protected. The Pas de Calais area, encompassing Calais and Boulogne, had numerous batteries including several heavy and super-heavy batteries, the best known being the four heavy naval batteries shown in the map at left.

In addition, there were other gun batteries in the area, some in casemates, others in open emplacements, plus bunkers, infantry strongpoints and other defences all along the coast, beginning at Bray-Dunes just across the border from Belgium, additionally inland there were more bunkers for radars and V-weapon sites.

Dunkerque's defences circled the town and included a variety of flak batteries, then extended down to Loon-Plage some 5km along the coast. This particular fortress would be not be captured when neighbouring Calais and Boulogne were taken by the Allied advance in the summer of 1944 and it had the doubtful distinction of being the last French town to be liberated on 10 May 1945.

In the Boulogne area at Wimereux (5km north) there was still a bunker from which, it is said, Hitler was to have watched Operation 'Sealion' in 1940. Festung Boulogne had been one of the first places to be designated as a fortress by the Führer and the town was ringed with gun batteries—both artillery and flak—infantry strongpoints and resistance nests. It had a 'surprisingly tenacious' garrison of about 10,000 men who would fight for six days, 17–22 September, despite being mainly from second-class fortress units. Operation 'Wellhit' was II Canadian Corps' attack on Boulogne which had cause to thank the 'Funnies' of 79th Armd Div, particularly the Crocodile flamethrowers who were most effective against bunkers.

Calais was heavily bombed by the RAF in late September and then captured by the Canadians once the specialised armour had been released from Boulogne. Operation 'Undergo', which took place between 25 September and 1 October, saw first Calais surrender on 30 September, following a truce to allow civilians to leave the city; and then the Cap Gris Nez batteries surrendered—thus ensuring that Boulogne's harbour could not be bombarded—on 29 September. Unlike other fortresses, the Calais Festung had not fought to the last man.

Above: *Hitler declared Boulogne a fortress. The harbour area was destroyed on 15 June, by an RAF raid that included Lancasters carrying 'Tallboy' bombs. At* **1** *StP Strandhafer, a heavy Flak position that protected the north side of the harbour—this is the garage for a Type L411A searchlight. At* **2** *WN228 Schlüsselblume, an SK Torpedo storage bunker.*

Left: *HKB Berck Nord was a three-gun battery and a defensive site on the north beach at Berck. Today it spills onto the beach and a number of bunkers have been demolished. Here, a V600v for a 5cm KwK.*

Below: *Part of Fort de Couppe, south of the city, StP Seerose was a battery of Mle 1910 SF 13.8cm guns housed in M270 casemates, the outline of one visible at* **1**. **2** *A Vf MG bunker. At* **3** *the Leitstand.*

Above: Today, Turm I of the four huge Battery Todt casemates, which housed 38cm guns, provides the setting for the Atlantic Wall Museum and outside the museum is a German Krupp K5 railway gun. The battery—originally named MKB Siegfried—was completed in January 1942 by Organisation Todt, the labour movement. The complex includes a number of personnel bunkers, Flak emplacements, ammunition bunkers, etc. This photo shows Turm III (left) and Turm IV.

Above Right: StP265 Lungenkraut. Near the village of Equihen, south of Boulogne, are the remains of five unusual SK bunkers, part of Luftwaffe long-range navigation system FuG 121 Erika. There's another of these sites at Saint-Pierre-Eglise on the Cotentin peninsula. By listening to the transmissions from the two stations aircraft could work out their precise positions (to within 400m). There are a number of Flak positions around the site.

Right: Between Equihen and Le Portel is Kriegsmarine Station Nessel. It has a V143 bunker which would have been equipped with a Mammut radar station. Alongside the V143 are two 622 bunkers for the crew and, as shown here, a Flak battery of six L401 bunkers that could take 8.8cm or 10.5cm AA guns, with a command post in the middle.

Main photo, A and D: StP120 Pommern at Wissant South used to be on dunes that were washed away by the waves. Today most of the bunkers have been demolished. Those shown here are a 630 and a 600—a stand for a 5cm KwK (**D**). Sketch based on info at www.maginot60.com. Pir6mon/WikiCommons/ CC BY-SA 3.0

B: StP143a Sickingen started as part of StP212 Frundsberg. The V143 base for a FuMo 51 Mammut radar (**1**) is flanked by two M270s (**2**) on top of Cap Gris Nez. There are two personnel bunkers (621 and 622) behind. There were three 17cm guns in the battery (Batterie Waringzelle), two in casemates and one in an open emplacement. Nearby, WN163 Wallenstein, a Kriegsmarine observation and radar strongpoint, included a Wellblech (**3**) and a Vf command post (**4**).

C: The Canadians took the big batteries on Cap Gris Nez and at Calais—this is the North Shore (New Brunswick) Regt at Sangatte. Lt Donald I. Grant/Canada. Dept. of National Defence/Library and Archives Canada/PA-133137

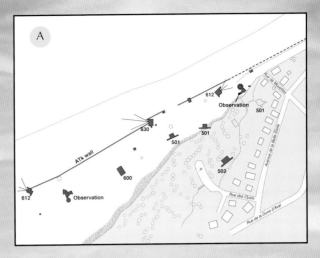

93

Right: One of the heaviest of the Pas de Calais batteries, this RAF PRU photograph shows Batterie Lindemann at Sangatte. Today the battery is buried under the spoil from the Channel Tunnel.

Below Right: StP107 Neuss—the Lindemann Battery, named in honour of the captain of the battleship Bismarck—had three 40.6cm SK C/34 guns in 17m high concrete emplacements. They fired over 2,000 shells across the Channel at Dover.

Below: Heavily bombed, the Lindemann Battery sustained little damage until one turret was hit on 3 September by a shell from a British railway gun.

Inset: Lt M.G. Aubut and Pte C.D. Walker of The North Shore Regiment examining a German cross-Channel gun, Sangatte, France, 26 September 1944. Lt Donald I. Grant/Canada. Dept. of National Defence/Library and Archives Canada/PA-133141

Left: *The defence of Calais was based on extensive flooded areas outside the city, heavy guns in position to guard the causeways and strong positions in the city itself—all made more formidable because they were isolated on islands in the many canals with liberal numbers of bunkers, guns in casemates and anti-tank guns all surrounded by mines and wire. On 17 September, the German garrison was around 5,000. The Canadians, however, had learned the recent lessons well and the use of bombing, artillery and armour (particularly the flamethrowers of 79th Armd Div) led to the surrender of the garrison on the 30th. USAF*

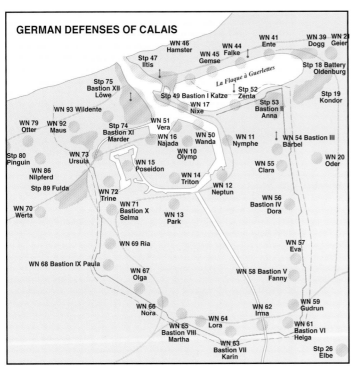

GERMAN DEFENSES OF CALAIS

WN 46 Hamster
Stp 47 Iltis
WN 44 Falke
WN 45 Gemse
WN 41 Ente
WN 39 Dogg
WN 2? Geier
Stp 18 Battery Oldenburg
Stp 75 Bastion XII Löwe
La Flaque à Guerlettes
Stp 49 Bastion I Katze
Stp 52 Zenta
Stp 53 Bastion II Anna
Stp 19 Kondor
WN 93 Wildente
WN 17 Nixe
WN 79 Otter
WN 92 Maus
Stp 74 Bastion XI Marder
WN 51 Vera
WN 16 Najada
WN 50 Wanda
WN 11 Nymphe
WN 54 Bastion III Bärbel
Stp 80 Pinguin
WN 73 Ursula
WN 10 Olymp
WN 20 Oder
WN 86 Nilpferd
WN 15 Poseidon
WN 55 Clara
Stp 89 Fulda
WN 14 Triton
WN 12 Neptun
WN 72 Trine
WN 71 Bastion X Selma
WN 13 Park
WN 56 Bastion IV Dora
WN 70 Werta
WN 69 Ria
WN 57 Eva
WN 68 Bastion IX Paula
WN 67 Olga
WN 58 Bastion V Fanny
WN 66 Nora
WN 62 Irma
WN 59 Gudrun
WN 64 Lora
WN 61 Bastion VI Helga
WN 65 Bastion VIII Martha
WN 63 Bastion VII Karin
Stp 26 Elbe

Above and Below: *WN79 (Otter) is to the west of Fort Lapin. Sinking slowly into the sand are two 612 casemates; behind them a large command post which was tied in to the various batteries—Lindemann, Oldenburg, Todt and Grosser Kurfürst—in the area.*

Above: *StP18, MKB Oldenburg, lies just east of Calais. As with the others in the chain that stretches to the Todt Battery south of Cap Gris Nez, construction of Oldenburg started in July 1940 when Operation 'Sea Lion', the invasion of England, was anticipated. The two open casemates (**A**, one shown **Below and Opposite, Below**) housed WWI-vintage Russian guns that Krupp had rechambered to 24cm. They could fire a 150kg projectile some 15 miles—short of the British coast but a danger to shipping. They had been captured near Libau in September 1915, transferred to Krupp who improved them and equipped them with gun shields. At the outbreak of war, the guns were employed on the island of* Borkum. *In 1940 they were transferred to the southern part of the Black Forest area to support the German invasion across the Rhine between Strasbourg and Mulhouse. Finally, in 1941 they were installed here on open emplacements with adjoining ammunition bunkers. In 1942 the casemates were enclosed and each gun was built into a specially-designed casemate with a height of 15m. The battery was equipped with state-of-the-art heat-sensitive sensors, as a result of which the battery could detect and attack shipping at night. During the war the camp—which can be seen outside the battery today—was used by the Organisation Todt.*

Top: *Coastal battery M1 Waldam of Marine Artillery Section 244 had three 15cm SK C/28 guns in two M270 casemates (**B**) and a unique revolving concrete cupola (SK Drehturm) which weighed 750 tons, installed on the rotating mechanism used to turn the main armament of the French battleship* Provence *(at* **C and Above***). Also shown are a three-level* Leistand *command post (at* **D and Above Left***), and a* Lichtsprech *bunker built to house equipment that used modulated light for communication (at* **E and Above Left***).*

Opposite: *This view looks from close to the Belgian border toward Dunkerque along the famous beaches from which the British evacuated in 1940. (Ship remains can still be seen at low tide [E].) There are many sites along this stretch of coast, many of them superimposed on top of earlier French defenses. Visible here are MKB Malo Terminus (A), built on top of a French fort that has its origins in the 18th century. Its Leitstand is seen at F and one of its casemates at H. Malo Terminus and Fort des Dunes were attacked and taken in June 1940. New bunkers and gun emplacements were built, four 671 casemates first equipped with 9.4cm Vickers Armstrong guns. These were replaced in June 1944 with 10.5cm guns. Fire control was provided by an M162a fire control post. Additionally there were various Flak and other gun positions. Fort des Dunes became Funkmeßortungsstellung Dahlie. Just north of the battery is a 219 Doppelschartenstand (C), an anti-tank casemate with two firing positions. At (D) is the 636 command post for a coastal battery (8th Battery Artillery Regt 18) of four 15.5cm guns inland at StP Delphin.*

G: *Today bunkers on the beach are used for art projects. This is WN Darmstadt near Leffrinckoucke.*

Below: *One of the iconic Atlantic Wall buildings: the Oye Plage Battery Leitstand.*

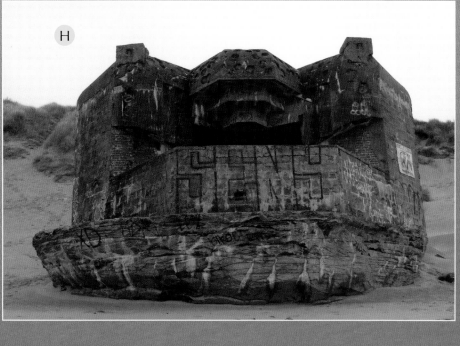

V- Weapons

The flying bomb campaign of 1944 was not just terrifying, sapping civilian morale, but did significant damage. 9,521 of the shorter-range V1s were fired at the UK June–October 1944, when the last site in range of Britain was overrun. Thereafter, they were directed at Antwerp and other targets in Belgium: 2,448 were launched up to 29 March 1945. The more deadly V2 was launched first against Paris on 8 September 1944, from a position in Belgium. By war's end, nearly 3,200 others had followed, killing c. 9,000 civilians and military personnel mainly in London, Antwerp, and Liege.

Unlike the V1s, the V2s were fired by mobile launchers which were difficult to locate. As an example, Art Abt 836 Bataillon (mot), set up in September 1943, began launching rockets on Lille and Mons on 14 September 1944, from the Euskirchen area shortly after moving across the Rhine to the Westerwald area, north of Montabaur. It fired 432 rockets from here—mainly at Antwerp and Liege—until the deteriorating military situation led to the unit fighting as infantry from 8 April 1945. Constructing the V2s killed more than their warheads, most of the dead from forced labour in the Dora-Mittelbau concentration camps around Nordhausen. The factory produced some 4,575 V2s between August 1944 and March 1945. Of the 60,000+ detainees employed in and around the complex 1943–45, 26,500 died.

Top Right: *Map showing the launching sites as identified in January 1944.*

Right and Below: *The characteristic ski slope launching ramps of the V1s were found all over northern France as the Allies advanced. From 80 to 100 such positions were erected up to the beginning of the invasion in 1944, between Calais and Le Havre.*

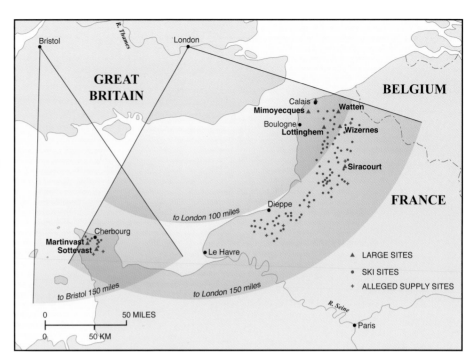

This Page: *Work started on this huge bunker—known as the Bunker of Eperlecques or the Watten bunker—in March 1943. It didn't take long for the Allies to realise that something was up and on 27 August it was bombed, the first of 25 occasions in the next year. By then it had become impossible to use the bunker as intended as a base to assemble and launch rockets. Through dint of hard work by slave labour and a lot of concrete, they were able to construct a factory for liquid oxygen. V2s were launched from mobile batteries which were less vulnerable to aerial attacks.* Velvet/Wiki Commons/ CC BY-SA 4.0 (Below and Bottom)

4 BELGIUM

As in the Netherlands, the Atlantic Wall on the Belgian coast comprised many bunkers and field works, backing up 37 battery sites along the 65km of North Sea coast. The great port of Antwerp and other ports such as Blankenberge, Zeebrugge, Oostende and Nieuwpoort (there were a total of 15 in all) were all protected by permanent fortifications and became *Verteidigungsbereich(en)* (VB) whilst the areas in between got much less attention. This, for example, reduced the number of bunkers built in Flanders to 160 (from a planned 399). In the end only 50 percent of the anticipated total was ever built and the hinterland was protected merely by barriers and small infantry bases. Rommel's inspection tour (on 21 December 1943) highlighted the shortcomings in this area.

The military organisation of the area fell to Fifteenth Armee under Gen Hans von Salmuth, whose HQ was in Tourcoing (France, near Lille). The army was made up of LXXXI and LXXXII (France), LXXXIX (Belgium and Netherlands) and LXVII (Reserve) Armeekorps. LXXXIX Armeekorps under General der Infanterie von und zu Gilsa was based in Antwerp and responsible for Walcheren, Noord-Beveland, and Zuid-Beveland in the Netherlands; the West Scheldt estuary; and Belgium.

There were two and a half 'fortresses' in Belgium—Oostende (a Stützpunktgruppe), Zeebrugge and the Scheldt, the latter including a chunk of Belgian soil. These fortresses had mixed fortunes: Oostende surrendered without a fight; Zeebrugge held out until 2 November, the last

Below: *The Atlantic Wall in Belgium—the main locations.*

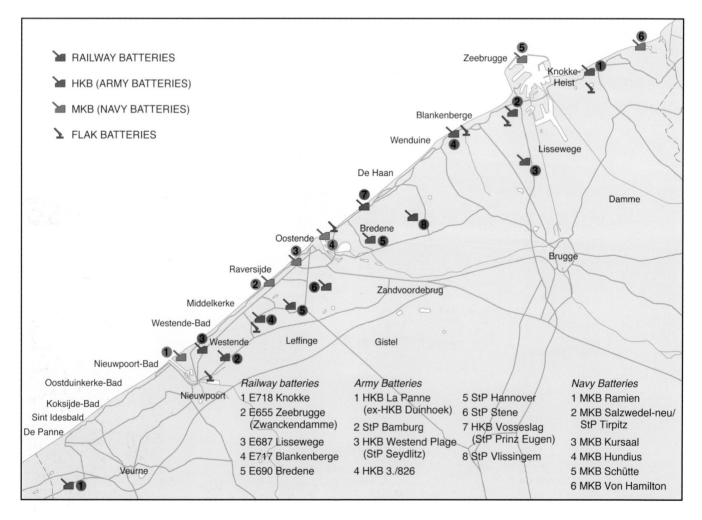

RAILWAY BATTERIES

HKB (ARMY BATTERIES)

MKB (NAVY BATTERIES)

FLAK BATTERIES

Zeebrugge
Knokke-Heist
Blankenberge
Wenduine
Lissewege
De Haan
Damme
Bredene
Oostende
Brugge
Raversijde
Zandvoordebrug
Middelkerke
Westende-Bad
Westende
Leffinge
Gistel
Nieuwpoort-Bad
Oostduinkerke-Bad
Nieuwpoort
Koksijde-Bad
Sint Idesbald
De Panne
Veurne

Railway batteries
1 E718 Knokke
2 E655 Zeebrugge (Zwanckendamme)
3 E687 Lissewege
4 E717 Blankenberge
5 E690 Bredene

Army Batteries
1 HKB La Panne (ex-HKB Duinhoek)
2 StP Bamburg
3 HKB Westend Plage (StP Seydlitz)
4 HKB 3./826
5 StP Hannover
6 StP Stene
7 HKB Vosseslag (StP Prinz Eugen)
8 StP Vlissingem

Navy Batteries
1 MKB Ramien
2 MKB Salzwedel-neu/ StP Tirpitz
3 MKB Kursaal
4 MKB Hundius
5 MKB Schütte
6 MKB Von Hamilton

part of Belgian soil to remain in German hands. The battle for the Scheldt was one of the hardest fought of all the battles on the northern front, with 12,873 Allied casualties, half of them from the Canadian forces involved.

Today, there are many vestiges of the Atlantic Wall in Belgium, particularly Raversijde Park outside Oostende. It not only contains the Saltzwedel neu/Tirpitz naval coastal battery of 6./MAA204 which formed part of the Atlantic Wall, but also the remains of WW1 German coastal defences and the Prince Karel Memorial. MKB Hundius at Oostende became the Cold War HQ of the Belgian Navy. It had four x 10.5cm SK L/40 guns in 671 gun bunkers.

Above Left: *Rommel and his staff inspect Raversijde.* Bundesarchiv, Bild 101I-295-1596-12/Kurth/CC-BY-SA 3.0

Above: *Head of the Nazi military government of Belgium from 1940 to 1944 was General der Infanterie Alexander von Falkenausen. On 18 July 1944, the Military Administration was replaced by a civil one, led by the Gauleiter, Josef Grohé, who was named the Reichskommissar of the Reichskommissariat of Belgium and Northern France. This position did not last long. The Allies' advance from the Normandy bridgehead meant that Belgium was liberated in September. Von Falkenausen was implicated in the 20 July Bomb Plot and spent the rest of the war in various concentration camps before being captured in the Tyrol by Fifth US Army on 5 May 1945. The headquarters of the LXXXIX Armeekorps was in Antwerp, the main CP being at Park den Brandt where two SK1 and a number of Vf bunkers remain. This is where the staff of General der Infanterie von und zu Gilsa were based until 29 August 1944, a few days before Antwerp was liberated by the Allies.* www.bunkerpictures.nl

Left: *Aerial PR photograph of Zeebrugge. The town and its 14,000 garrison was under Generalmajor Knut Eberding, CO of 64th Infanterie Division. It held out until 1 November.* USAF

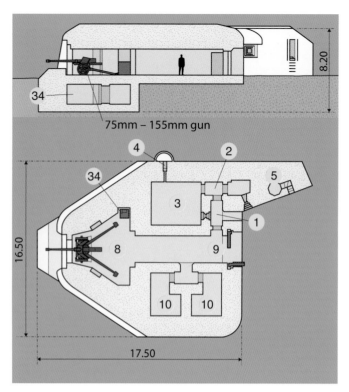

75mm – 155mm gun

Adinkerke

StP49 Schlieffen at Adinkerke was a four-gun 15.5cm battery housed in 611 casemates with a 610 command bunker. The original HKB had six 15.5cm K 418 (f) guns on open emplacements but this was moved to the coast to become HKB La Panne. The position was taken over by a battery of AR252 (171. Infanterie Div) and captured by the Canadians on 012 September 1944. Partially demolished postwar, one 611 has disappeared and another is ruined.

Below: *Partially demolished 611. Today the site is protected.*

Bottom and Left: *Plan and rear view of a 611. Note the original wooden door through which the 15.5cm gun was inserted; the main entrance is next to it on the right. The Scharte of the Nahkampfraum has been blocked off. At right the entrance to the Tobruk.*

Both photos Jente de Roust/Traces of War

Nieuwpoort

Top: *View through machine-gun slit of a German strongpoint showing beach defences north of Nieuwpoort. Canada. Dept. of National Defence/Library and Archives Canada*

Above and Below: *The first thing that strikes the visitor to StP16 Bamburg in Lombardsijde (a suburb of Nieuwpoort) is that the bunkers aren't dug in as usual and that the trenches are brick-lined. The reason is simple: as with so much of the land along this coast, the watertable is high and is historically a problem.*

Because of this, the bunkers were built tough. The battery of four 105mm weapons was originally in open emplacements but in 1944 work had started on concrete structures made from blocks rather than poured concrete. There are many bunkers to be seen including a 502 personnel bunker (not illustrated), an 610 command bunker with a reinforced Tobruk visible on top (Above) and an 669 (Below). Both Bjorn Gonsaeles/Traces of War

Above: *StP Seydlitz was the well-defended location of HKB Westend-Plage with six 15.5cm 418 (f) guns in open emplacements and a plethora of bunkers and tunnels. The Canadian Essex Scottish Regt/2nd Inf Div took it after heavy fighting 10–12 September 1944. This Vf for personnel has an entrance protected by brick walls.* Willy Vereenooghe

Raversijde

Right and Opposite: *The magnificent Domein Raversijde museum, just to the west of Oostende Airport not only contains MKB Saltzwedel neu/ Tirpitz, but also the remains of the WW1 German coastal defence battery Aachen and the Prince Karel Memorial. It has well over 60 bunkers and batteries from both world wars.*

Inset Left: *This rangefinder can be seen near the WW1 command post at C in top photo p108.*

Opposite, Above: *One of the 671 casemates introduced in April 1944.*

Opposite, Inset Left: *Replica of the four captured Belgian 12cm guns, designated 12cm K 370 (b), installed in 1941.*

Opposite, Inset Right: *A flanking 612 casemate for a 7.5cm PaK, as seen here.* Raversijde images by Paul Hermans/WikiCommons

Above: *Rommel and his staff inspect MKB Tirpitz.* Bundesarchiv, Bild 101I-295-1596-09/Kurth/CC-BY-SA 3.0

Right, Far Right, Opposite Centre and Below: *Internal views of the museum showing living conditions inside the bunkers.* Dennis Jarvis/WikiCommons/CC BY-SA 2.0

Opposite, Above and Below: *The magnificent Domein Raversijde museum, just to the west of Oostende Airport. With well over 60 bunkers and batteries from both world wars, it was preserved by Prince Karel (1903–83), Count of Flanders and Regent of Belgium 1944–50, who lived here (house at* **E**) *from 1950.* **B** *is the entrance to the museum. Among the goodies on show are the WWI Aachen Battery (***A***);* **C** *is a WWI fire control post with a rangefinder in front (see p. 107). The WWII battery was initially named MKB Saltzwedel neu but later called Tirpitz.* **D** *Various different anti-tank and anti-landing craft obstacles used on the beaches of the Atlantic Wall.* **F** *House used by battery commander.* **G** *(left, right, and photo Top Right on p. 107) two of the four 671 bunkers built.* **H** *WWII observation bunker and command post.*

Oostende

Inset, Opposite: *West of the entrance to Oostende harbour lies Fort Napoleon (A) which was built in 1811. In both world wars it became the HQ for German artillery in the area. Oostende harbour was well defended. At B1 (and Inset, Centre) the most easterly casemate of Battery Hundius; this 671 would have housed a 10.5cm gun.*

Main photo: *Oostende had its fair share of defenses— including those identified here, part of PzStP Hafen that protected the harbour and locks: B Battery Hundius, with its M157 fire control post (B2, inset) and four 671 casemates (A1). C Halve Maan Battery, which had a number of emplacements for guns and Flak (see also overleaf). D An 633 bunker whose main armament was a 5cm M19 mortar (see p36) underneath a heavy armoured steel cupola, with a range of 750m. There's also a special transformer building that handled the town's electricity (E).*

Above: *The German anti-aircraft battery of the Halve Maan. At left the L421A command post.* Marc Ryckaert/WikiCommons/ CC BY 3.0

Opposite, Centre: *One of the Hundius Battery 671 casemates.* Marc Ryckaert/WikiCommons/ CC BY 3.0

Opposite, Below: *StP Kolberg lies just outside the village of Stene along the former anti-tank ditch at the Schorredijk/Schorrestraat. An official monument since 1998, it was part of the landside defence of Oostende and was made up of two 669 casemates (one shown at **Left**), and an open emplacement.* Marc Ryckaert/ WikiCommons/ CC BY 3.0

Below Left: *There are also two 630 MG emplacements (as here) and an 667 for a 5cm KwK. These were part of WN Wolf.* www.bunkerpictures.nl (Above Left and Below Left)

Above and Below: *This 636 is the only survivor of StP Von der Goltz/Bruch-müller north of Oostende. It was there to direct the fire of* Eisenbahnbatterie E690—four 28cm kurze Bruno Kanone *railway guns. There was another director at Raversijde. Plan of a typical 636 shown* **Below**. www.bunkerpictures.nl

Below Right: *The sole remaining bunker of PzStP Blaue Schleuse, defending the east of Oostende, is a 505 PaK casemate for 3.7cm with armoured plate. No longer in green fields it is surrounded by Bredene Shopping Centre. Unusually, the original steel armour plate is still in place.* www.bunkerpictures.nl (right); Willy Vereenooghe

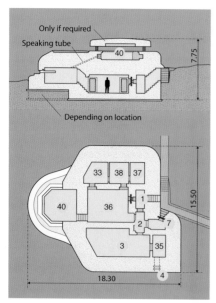

Blankenberge

Above: *Blankenberge harbour: not many of the defences remain—a 680 (**A** and **inset**) emplacement for a 7.5cm anti-tank gun and a Tobruk for an FT17 turret (**B**).* Marc Ryckaert/WikiCommons/ CC BY 3.0 (Inset)

Left, Far Left and Below: *Blankenberge beaches in 1944 were protected by ATk walls, ditches, barbed-wire entanglements and camouflage netting. The town was liberated in early September 1944.* NARA; Canada. Dept. of National Defence/Library and Archives Canada

4 THE NETHERLANDS

The commander of all German troops in Fortress Holland was Luftwaffe General der Flieger Friedrich Christiansen, known as 'Krischan', one of the very few Luftwaffe officers who became a theatre/country commander. In fact, Rommel's Armeegruppe B dealt direct with Generaloberst Hans Reinhardt's LXXXVIII Armeekorps (374th and 719th Inf Divs and 16th Luftwaffe Fd Div), which was responsible for the wall from the River Scheldt to the Dutch/German border. In addition 70th Inf Div of Fifteenth Army, which had been formed on Walcheren in 1944, was given the nickname of the 'white bread division', because so many of its soldiers had stomach problems, they needed special rations. Nevertheless they would fight extremely bravely when attacked by the British and Canadians in November 1944.

In the north, the coastline was protected by the West Frisian and Wadden Islands which masked the Waddenzee and Ijsselmeer, making it difficult to get to the important city of Amsterdam. Den Helder, at the northern end of the North Holland peninsula, was declared a fortress on 8 July 1941 so was heavily fortified. It had long been a naval base, while just to its east was Den Oever at the western end of the Ijsselmeer Barrier Dam which had been completed in 1932. At that time defensive works, including road blocks, had been built, plus nearly 20 bunkers, earthworks and such like at Kornwerderzand. The Germans constructed three additional bunkers here and also more to guard the eastern end of the dam.

Further down the coast there were many fortifications. Ijmuiden had also been declared a fortress as had the Hoek van Holland. Between the Hoek and Rotterdam, the island of Rozenburg had some formidable coastal batteries defending the seaway to Rotterdam. Finally, there was the island of Walcheren—on which Vlissingen (Flushing) had been given fortress status—and the area on the south bank of the Scheldt, Zeeuws-Vlaanderen centered on Terneuzen. For the civilian population, the worst consequence was the growing number of forced evacuations, such as that of most of the inhabitants of Walcheren. The German fixed defences on Walcheren were formidable, with 18 major coastal batteries, supplemented inshore with field artillery weapons and anti-tank guns. Many of the farmhouses had been made into strongpoints with all the usual field defences, including minefields and flamethrowers. At Vlissingen there were also torpedo batteries. The garrison was 10,000-men strong. Backing up the land garrison was a flotilla of some 85 small warships, again mainly based at Vlissingen. The Walcheren fortifications and the other defences held the key to the opening up of the Scheldt estuary which would unlock the major port of Antwerp.

The forced evacuations of civilians from the coastal areas continued, being especially serious in the densely inhabited coastal zone around Rotterdam and The Hague. Thousands of civilians had to move and many buildings were demolished. This caused great unrest, especially as the rumours were that a 50km belt of fortifications was to be constructed in the coastal area. Fortunately this turned out to be an exaggeration. Nevertheless, as an example, the creation of StPGr Scheveningen saw nearly 3,500 buildings destroyed and 135,000 people moved out. On top of

Top: *The use of Eastern troops in the Netherlands was not hugely successful — they were not completely in tune with their German masters as was shown on Texel between 5 April and 20 May 1945 when the Georgians — 882. Infanterie Bataillon Königin Tamara, posted to the island that February — rebelled.*

Above: *Commando memorial on Uncle Beach at Vlissingen on Walcheren.*

this, the local inhabitants were forced to work in helping to build fortifications.

There were over 60 batteries where coastal artillery guns were located, of varying calibres up to 24cm. Also stationed in the Netherlands were seven naval artillery detachments (201–206 and 607) and six naval AA detachments (246, 703, 808, 810, 813 and 816), plus two port protection flotillas, four river flotillas and a boom defence flotilla (*Netzsperrflotille*) .

What can be seen today?

There is still much to see of the Atlantic Wall, particularly on Walcheren and on the coast between the Hook of Holland and Den Helder: the island of Ijmuiden is a UNESCO World Heritage Site and so protected. There are a number of active preservation societies—such as the Stichting Bunkerbehoud, amongst whose projects include the Bunker 621 Abeele (see p120) and the restoration of the German Type 143 observation bunker on the mole at Vlissingen (see p118).

Above Right: *Arthur Seyss-Inquart was the leader of the Austrian National Socialists and after the Anschluss ran the new German province of Ostmark—what Austria became when it was incorporated into the Reich. Later he served in the General Government of Occupied Poland before being appointed Reichskommissar for the Occupied Netherlands in May 1940. He was hanged after being found guilty of crimes against humanity at the Nuremberg Trials.*

Right: *Arthur Seyss-Inquart's bunker—part of StPGr Clingendael—was heavily disguised as a farmhouse: the chimneys were positions for Flak Vierlings.*

Below: *Walcheren has a remarkable number of bunkers. These two 611s and four open emplacements formed StP Hotzendörf outside Westkapelle. They were inundated after the RAF burst the dykes. Note, as is usual on Walcheren (because of the high watertable), the ammo bunkers are outside the casemates rather than under them.*

Walcheren and Zeeland

The attack on Walcheren, heavily defended with many prepared positions, was essential to the clearing of the Scheldt estuary to bring Antwerp harbour into use. Operation 'Infatuate' started with an RAF bombing attack on the island's dykes on the night of 3 October to flood the Germans out of the interior. Unfortunately, information about the raid didn't reach the villagers in Westkapelle (**Above**) and 180 were killed. The damaged dyke wasn't finally repaired until 12 October 1945. The breaching of the dykes meant that the Germans had to vacate many of their bunkered positions in the interior of the island, but stiffened the defense around the coast. The Allies attacked at Westkapelle and Vlissingen (Flushing) on 1 November. By the 8th the island was liberated.

Left: During the operation, 30 of the Close Support Squadron landing craft were lost to accurate fire from the coastal batteries: over 300 were killed in the action. NARA

Right and Below: Vlissingen and the Walcheren Canal. At **A** (and **Below Left**) the newly restored observation bunker. No. 4 Commando landed just east of this. **B** is the location of the Commando memorial seen on p116. **C** (and **Below**) one of the harbour defences, a 630 MG bunker with an armoured shield. **D** is Middelburg, capital of Zeeland. www.bunkerpictures.nl (both below)

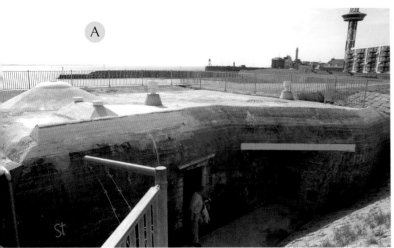

A

C

Above and Right: *Part of VB Vlissingen, on the corner of the New Vlissingseweg and Abeelseweg, stands a fascinating restoration project. This 621, the command post for the area, was camouflaged with a false roof and painted to resemble a suburban house. Recently restored by the Stichting Bunkerbehoud, once again it blends into its surroundings. The Province of Zeeland (Above); Stichting Bunkerbehoud (Right)*

Below Right: *Built in a corner of an anti-tank ditch, part of the landside defences of VB Vlissingen is the only remaining 680 on Walcheren, a casemate for a flanking 7.5cm PaK 40.*

Opposite: *One of the main reasons to inundate Walcheren was the sheer number of defensive structures on the island. As well as the coastal defences, over 200 bunkers studded the interior, including a number of areas designated strongpoints. The one pictured here, between Vlissingen and Koudekerke, was set up as StP Kolberg and its defenses included an anti-tank ditch, dragon's teeth, and bunkers to shelter troops, store water, prepare meals and care for the injured. In contrast to the fortifications on higher ground, StP Kolberg never had to be actively defended because it was inundated. **1** is a 631 armed with a 47mm anti-tank gun. **2, 3, 4 (and plan inset)** are of Type 623 armed with machine guns—Regelbau Bunker vom Typ 623 MG Schartenstand mit Vorsatzplatte (60°).*

1 One of two surviving 502 personnel bunkers of WN Eschwege, in Ritthem east of Vlissingen.

2 The HQ of the German forces defending Walcheren and Beveland was in Toorenvliedt, a southwestern suburb of Middelburg. Bunkers had been built there from 1942 but the breaking of the dykes led to their inundation and they had to be vacated on 17 October. This is the divisional communications bunker, a 618, that is being painstakingly restored by Stichting Bunkerbehoud.

3 StP Fichte was the site of Marineflakbatterie Nord in the West Souburg suburb of Vlissingen. It was equipped with four 10.5cm SK C/32 guns. Today there are two Fla14a bunkers and this personnel bunker. Following the RAF's breaching of the dykes, the site would have been inundated were it not for local efforts — in vain, however; the site was bombed and played no part in the land battle.

4 *This unusual bunker is a Type 700, a casemate for a 7.5cm PaK 40 with an armoured ceiling plate 22cm thick thus allowing a lower silhouette than those with thicker concrete rooves.*

5, 6 *Burgh-Haamstede is the capital of the island of Schouwen-Duiveland, north of Walcheren. This command bunker—Type 117a with a 486P2 observation Panzerturm—is part of WN325H a position of more than 20 bunkers.*

7 *On the west coast of Walcheren, between Zoutelande and Biggekerke, is StP Von Seeckt—two 611 casemates (the front of one seen here) whose fire control was a Type 143 at WN Carmen.*

8 *This is a 638 hospital bunker at Haamstede on Schouwen-Duiveland.*

9 *Schouwen-Duiveland was not as heavily defended as Walcheren, but still had its fair share of bunkers. This observation tower is near StP 43H on the coast.*

All photos on this spread www.bunkerpictures.nl

Above: *Strategically placed on the south side of Hollands Diep, Willemstad was built in the late 16th century. Today, the modern bridge from Schouwen-Duiveland reaches the mainland nearby.* During the war it was Batteriestellung Willemstad, StP XXXIV H, and there were two 669s (**A**) built on Bastion Holland, an observation bunker (**B**) on Bastion Gelderland and various other emplacements including three Tobruks and an anti-tank wall. Rijksdienst voor het Cultureel Erfgoed (Aerial); G.Lanting/WikiCommons/ CC BY-SA 3.0 (Bastion noticeboards)

Right: *Recently excavated 502 personnel bunker with a Flak position on the roof at Willemsdorp, south of Dordrecht.*

Left and Below Left: WN220H at Ouddorp on the island Goeree-Overflakkee. In 2010 a group of volunteers began excavating and developing the complete Widerstandsnest. They have done a marvellous job and for their work won the Dutch bunker award 'De gouden Betonmolen' in 2012. Here, a Tobruk for an MG (**Left**) and an anti-tank gun position (**Below Left**).

Below: WN222H, also at Ouddorp, was renovated some years ago with help from EU funds. There's an emplacement for a 4.7cm anti-tank gun.

All colour photos on this spread www.bunkerpictures.nl

Hoek van Holland

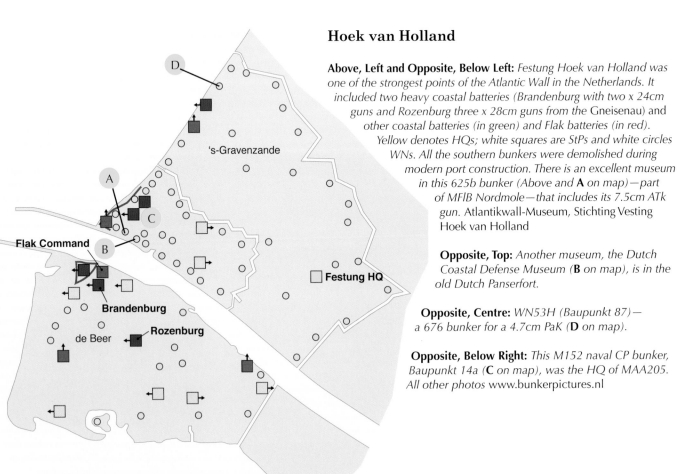

Above, Left and Opposite, Below Left: *Festung Hoek van Holland was one of the strongest points of the Atlantic Wall in the Netherlands. It included two heavy coastal batteries (Brandenburg with two x 24cm guns and Rozenburg three x 28cm guns from the Gneisenau) and other coastal batteries (in green) and Flak batteries (in red). Yellow denotes HQs; white squares are StPs and white circles WNs. All the southern bunkers were demolished during modern port construction. There is an excellent museum in this 625b bunker (Above and* **A** *on map)—part of MFlB Nordmole—that includes its 7.5cm ATk gun. Atlantikwall-Museum, Stichting Vesting Hoek van Holland*

Opposite, Top: *Another museum, the Dutch Coastal Defense Museum (* **B** *on map), is in the old Dutch Panserfort.*

Opposite, Centre: *WN53H (Baupunkt 87)— a 676 bunker for a 4.7cm PaK (* **D** *on map).*

Opposite, Below Right: *This M152 naval CP bunker, Baupunkt 14a (* **C** *on map), was the HQ of MAA205. All other photos www.bunkerpictures.nl*

Above and Right: *StPGr Scheveningen included MSB Scheveningen-Nord, just north of Ostduin, armed initially with six French 15.5cm guns and later with four 15cm SK C/28 guns housed in 671 SK casemates (**Right**) built in spring 1944. This well-preserved battery is well connected by trenches and has an S414 fire control bunker (**Above** with the Scheveningen pier in the background). There were six 501 personnel bunkers, an M151 CP and two Fl246 ammunition bunkers and many other buildings including Flak positions, radar, kitchen, water tanks, medical, barracks etc. There were a number of bunkers to defend against an attack: the front was covered by two 612 field gun bunkers; the rear by a 667 (5cm KwK) and two casemates for field guns along with a tank wall. The Stichting Atlantikwall Museum Scheveningen identifies the personnel in August 1944 to be: 8./MAA201, with two officers, 24 NCOs and 125 men; 4./Festungstormtruppen, of five men; 2./SS-Panzer Jäger, with two officers and 15 men; FluWa, consisting of one NCO and five men. www.bunker-pictures.nl*

Right: *This Type 600 bunker was unearthed as part of an artwork. It's at Duindorp, a southern suburb of The Hague. Local historians say it wasn't used as an artillery position but as an HQ for a police battalion. Loki2003/Fotothing/ (CC BY 2.5*

Left: *Stichting Atlantikwall Museum Scheveningen is based in this 608 bunker (a Battalion, Departmental or regimental CP). Nearby there's a 622 Doppelgruppenunterstand. From the 608 bunker and the nearby villas the military command ran StPGr Scheveningen — eight StPs and 3 WNs.* Vincent van Zeijst/ WikiCommons/ CC BY-SA 3.0

Below Left and Below: *Further north up the coast lies StPGr Katwijk. There were a number of casemates and bunkers, many today covered with sand, but there are some still visible: a tank wall on the southern side studded with Vf MG bunkers and a well-preserved Höckerlinie dragon's teeth barrier (**Left**); two SK emplacements for a 17cm gun and a 607 ammo bunker, all part of Batterie Katwijk Alt; Flak batterie Witte Berg; and by Valkenburg Airport a 616 communications bunker.* Janericloebe/WikiCommons

Ijmuiden

Right: *Ijmuiden, the gateway to Amsterdam, was declared a fortress. It was protected by four Flak and three artillery batteries — one to the south, one to the north and one on Forteiland (Fort Island).*

Below and Opposite: *Fort Island was created at the mouth of the North Sea Canal around 1885 and today is a World Heritage Site. Few of the WWII defences remain following reworking of the island in the 1960s—of the original 24 bunkers three 644s (one shown here at* **A** *with a Sechss- chartenturm that would have been armed with two MG34s), five 631s, two 633s, a 191 and a M170 were removed; a 636 and two 611s were demolished too. Those remaining include:* **B** *671SK modified to take a British 9.4cm naval gun and* **C** *a VF for launching depth charges if a submarine tried to penetrate the harbour defences. Ad Meskens/WikiCommons (Below; Opposite, Top); www.bunkerpictures.nl (p131 inset top and Below and Bottom Right)*

C   D

B

*The most southerly of the batteries that protected Ijmuiden, WN81 Seeziel Batterie Heerenduin's four x 21cm guns were originally in open emplacements. By July 1944 four M272s had replaced them (**A–D** above; note free-standing tunnel airshaft behind this casemate); two Fl246 ammunition bunkers and a 612 on the beach were also added. In the centre of the battery stands an imposing M178 fire-control post (Leitstand) (**E**) which wasn't ready for action when the fortress surrenderded in 1945. To the south of Heer-enduin is a Flak battery. The site also houses a museum, which has renovated some of the trench system. It also has a section devoted to the Seehund midget submarines (see p134).* Janericloebe/Wi-kiCommons (all)

Opposite, Below: *South of Heerenduin lies WN82 MFlB Olmen. Comprising two Fl243 and two Fl249 positions for heavy 10.5cm Flak, there is also an Fl244 Flak Leitstand (seen here without its rangefinder and armoured cover) and two Fl246 ammunition bunkers.* www.bunkerpictures.nl

C

S-boot pens were built at a number of locations on the Channel coast including Ostende, Rotterdam, Cherbourg and Boulogne. Two large pens were built at Ijmuiden, construction of the first starting in autumn 1940 and the second in 1943, increasing capacity to 42 boats. Heavily bombed by the USAAF and RAF, the pens nevertheless survived intact. (**Opposite, Top:** B-26 bombing Ijmuiden. Note at **A** the 1944 shape of Fort Island seen previously.) After the war, SBB I was torn down to its foundations but SBB II (seen **Above** and at **B**) with its slanted walls was spared.

Right: Ijmuiden was also used by the Kriegsmarine's remarkably unsuccessful midget submarine forces. These are Type XXVII Seehund submarines, 24 of which went to Ijmuiden by the end of December 1944. Their operational debut was New Year's Day 1945 when 17 sailed from Ijmuiden to attack a convoy off the Kwinte Bank. Of these David Hallas of uboat.net reported, '7 found beached. 2 returned. 1 sunk by HMS Cowdray. 1 sunk by HMS Ekins. 1 abandoned at Domberg. 1 found drifting by an MTB. 4 disappeared. Probably bad weather.' The solitary success was the sinking of the trawler Hayburn Wyke. Hallas's summary of Seehund operations in 1945 is: 'In total 142 sorties — this resulted in the loss of nine ships totalling 18,451 tons sunk and three ships of 18,354 tons damaged. 35 Seehund were lost.'
Canada. Dept. of National Defence/ Library and Archives Canada (Above Right); Hanno Lans/WikiCommons/ CC BY 2.0 (Right and opposite); USAF (Opposite, Top)

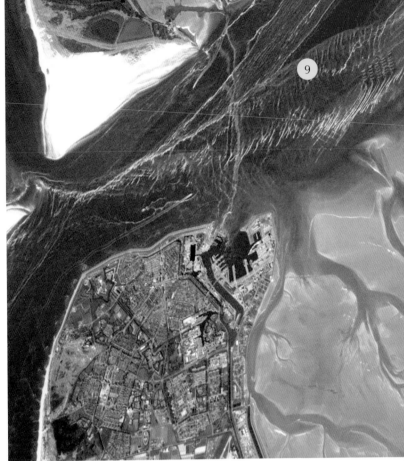

1 *Fortress Ijmuiden had a well-defended landward side. This anti-tank wall was part of WN82 and 83, Battery Olmen. Janericloebe/Wiki-Commons (1, 3, 4)*

2 *Aerial view showing water-filled anti-tank ditches. The circles denote portable ATk guns. USAF*

3 *WN92, an unusual gate in the anti-tank wall.*

4 *R58 Tobruk, part of WN83 and 84.*

Den Helder

Den Helder in the northern Netherlands has been the home port of the Dutch Royal Navy for over 175 years. It was well-defended by the Germans, identified as a Verteidigungsbereich. Its strategic importance meant it had many old Dutch forts and defences that were taken over by the occupying forces.

5 *Undergrowth appearing from the escape shaft of this 621 personnel bunker in the southern landward defence line near Julianadorp. www.bunkerpictures.nl (5, 6, 7, 8)*

6 *This M219, part of Seezielbatterie Zanddijk, was once equipped with a turret containing a 15cm SK C/28 from the battleship Gneisenau.*

7 *FL246 of MFlB Dirksz Admiraal, WN120M, an old fort originally built by the French 1811–13 which became an AA battery armed with four 10.5 cm SK C/32 guns.*

8 *This FL250 Flugabwehrgruppencommandostand, WN123a, is nick-named the 'Kroontjesbunker' (crowned bunker).*

9 *This view is from the International Space Station and shows the strait between Den Helder and the island of Texel at low tide in 2007. NASA*

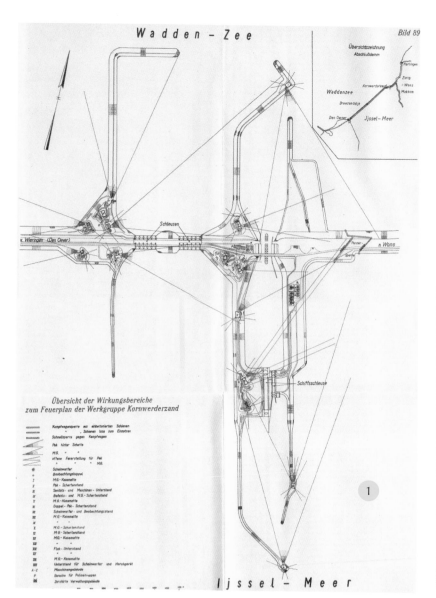

Wadden-Zee

Bild 89

Übersicht der Wirkungsbereiche
zum Feuerplan der Werkgruppe Kornwerderzand

Ijssel-Meer

R 7000

1942

Kornwerderzand

Linking Friesland with North Holland, the Afsluitdijk was constructed between 1927 and 1933. Kornwerderzand lies on an artificial island created during the construction of the dam which runs from Den Oever in North Holland to Zurich in Friesland. Fortified originally by the Dutch, the fortifications are split up into two lines and contain 17 Dutch casemates built 1928–31. The Germans took over the fortifications and some additional bunkers and other smaller defense works were constructed.

1 Map of Kornwerderzand showing the arcs of fire from the gun emplacements.

2 Aerial view of Kornwerderzand; at **A** an MG bunker.

3 Kazemat V—Dutch-built MG casemate. www.bunkerpictures.nl (3, 4, 5, 6, 7)

4, 5 Internal and external view of 5cm anti-tank gun in a 667 bunker.

6 2cm Flak emplacement.

7 Dutch Kazemat VI, with two 5cm guns.

The West Frisian Islands

Right: *Texel Lighthouse was the epicentre of the Georgian Uprising of April 1945 when the occupying force—the 882nd Infantry Battalion Königin Tamara from the Georgian Soviet Socialist Republic—rebelled against the Germans. They gained control of the tiny island, but were unable to hold it against German reinforcements. The last group defended the lighthouse. The fighting continued until 20 May—two weeks after the war ended.* Jan Anskeit/WikiCommons/ CC BY-SA 3.0

Below: *Texel airfield was extended by the Germans. This is the Fliegerhorst gefechtsstand—Vf command post.* www.bunkerpictures.nl

Left: *StP 12H is a bunker complex on the island of Vlieland. It is being renovated and should make an interesting tourist attraction when it opens.* MarcoSwart/WikiCommons/ CC BY-SA 4.0

Below: *WN9M—MFlB Terschelling West—was part of the StPGr Terschelling and consisted of four heavy AA guns and other bunkers such as the Tobruk seen here.* Arch/ WikiCommons

Below, Inset: *StP XI is the Marine Battery Den Hoorn. This is the Dutch-built CP.* China_Crisis/ WikiCommons/CC BY-SA 2.5

Opposite, Bottom: *StPGr Texel, WN21a De Dennen had a range of bunkers. This one is a protected garage.* www. bunkerpictures.nl

5 DENMARK AND NORTH GERMANY

Below: *The main Atlantic Wall locations in Denmark. There were nine naval artillery detachments, four naval AA detachments and two naval artillery arsenals in Denmark.*

Main photo: *North of Søndervig is an important fortification that consists of 50 bunkers and another 50 installations. The bunkers would also have been protected by minefields and barbed-wire entanglements. This is the 636 fire control post for HKB 5./180. Kurt Lund Mogensen (KLM)*

Swiftly occupying Denmark in the spring of 1940, the Germans immediately began to fortify the coastline so as to ensure direct links with their troops in Norway. *Befehlshaber der deutsches Truppen in Dänemark* (Head of the Occupation Forces in Denmark) was Generalleutnant Hermann von Hanneken from 27 September 1942 until 27 January 1945 when he handed over to Generaloberst Georg Lindemann who surrendered Armee Lindemann at the end of the war.

Von Hanneken had specific orders to bolster coastal defences against a possible invasion. The Germans thought that this would be on the flanks of one of the harbours that the Allies would have to capture. Coastal defences were, therefore, reinforced in these places and thinned out elsewhere along the open coast. It was also necessary to fortify the land-bridges that led inland from the countless small fishing villages, through the dunes and then over the boggy areas behind them. A major expansion began in 1943, when the Heer and Kriegsmarine began a systematic extension of coastal defences from the German border up to Skagen and round to Frederikshavn.

Along this line infantry strongpoints and other field defences were built in long chains. The key points in the coastal defence were: Frederikshavn, Skagen, Løkken, Hanstholm, the entrance to Limfjord, Søndervig, Blåvand and Esbjerg, with Hanstholm and Esbjerg being the strongest. In total there were 78 batteries with some 300-plus guns of varying calibres, two of the largest being the 38cm guns at Oksby and Esbjerg. There were also, as in Norway, some torpedo batteries in concrete shelters.

At the time of D-Day the Danish invasion defences were still incomplete and that summer and autumn the

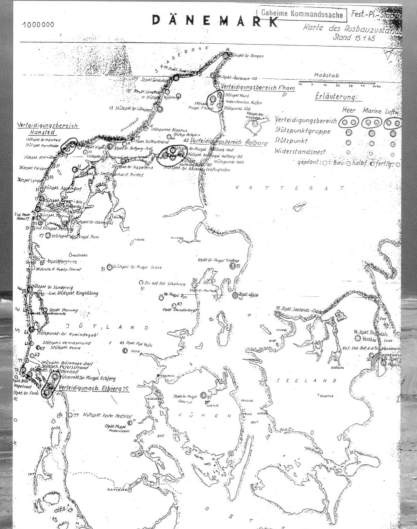

Kriegsmarine warned of the potential danger of an attack in the Skagerrak and Kattegat, which could allow the Allies to penetrate into the Baltic. This would isolate Norway and have a serious effect upon submarine warfare, especially if Sweden joined in on the Allied side. Accordingly, a series of batteries was built in the east of Jutland and on the coasts of Funen and Zealand. Most of these were just basic field works containing few concrete structures. However, it was felt that without them more troops would be needed to defend Denmark, whilst it would be highly dangerous to open up such an inviting route into Germany.

Peter Christensen said in his book *Coast Fortifications in Denmark*:

'The German works in Denmark exhibit great variety of design and construction varying in size from the small flanking positions that are found along most of Jutland's west coast to the large fort-like structures that were placed around Esbjerg, Hanstholm and Frederikshavn. The flanking positions normally consist of three bunkers while the three fortified towns just mentioned consist of around 1,300, 700 and 300 respectively. In all the Germans built more than 7,000 bunkers in Denmark. The number of fortified groups or areas is also very large. For instance, the combined number of just the coast defence batteries, anti-aircraft batteries and radar stations comes to more than 150. In addition there are infantry strongpoints of various sizes, flanking positions, various technical installations etc., in all more than 300 fortified areas.'

Germany

The small length of North Sea coastline of Germany, stretching from the Danish border to the Dutch border, contained significant German ports and naval bases, such as Hamburg, Bremerhaven, Wilhelmshaven and Cuxhaven, all of which were heavily garrisoned, protected and difficult to capture. This was made even more difficult by the fortification of the off-shore East Frisian Islands, which were garrisoned and protected with

numerous gun batteries. The area of the German Bight, for example, had some 50 gun batteries, which included at least 12 heavy guns of 24cm calibre or over.

The naval artillery presence was considerable, and was divided under two headquarters until late 1944. These were the Naval Command North Sea and Coastal Command German Bight (later known as the Admiral German Bight). Under their command were numerous naval and AA artillery regiments and detachments, plus port protection flotillas and other units. As an example of the considerable numbers involved, here are the units listed as under command of Naval Command North Sea:

Above: *A meeting of the Danish-German Association in 1941. From left: Hinrich Lohse, who was Oberpräsident (High President) of the Province of Schleswig-Holstein; Thorvald Stauning, who was Prime Minister of Denmark until his death on 3 May 1942; Cecil von Renthe-Fink was the German ambassador to Denmark and became plenipotentiary of Denmark on 9 April 1940. He was superseded in 1942 by Dr Werner Best; and Peter Knutzen (chairman). WikiCommons*

Below: *There were over 4,500 Germans on Helgoland (or Heligoland) at the end of the war. The U-boat pens emerged relatively undamaged and were subsequently demolished by the British. Pegasus2 /WikiCommons/CC BY-SA 3.0*

- Borkum Island—a port protection flotilla, one naval artillery detachment and one naval AA detachment.
- Emden (covering the five most northerly Dutch provinces)—a naval AA regiment with six naval AA detachments, plus two reserve AA detachments and a naval motor transport detachment.
- Norderney—one naval artillery detachment and one naval AA detachment.
- Wangerooge—two naval artillery detachments, one naval AA detachment and one training detachment for AA guns.
- Wilhelmshaven—a port protection flotilla, a naval AA regiment (later renamed Marineflak Brigade), with seven naval AA detachments, including two AA floating batteries on the Medusa and Niobe, one naval artillery detachment and other units.

- Wesermünde (Bremerhaven)—two naval AA detachments.
- Helgoland—one naval artillery detachment, one naval AA detachment.
- Cuxhaven—a port protection flotilla, one naval AA detachment and one naval artillery reserve detachment.
- Brunsbüttel—naval AA regiment with four AA detachments.
- Sylt—five naval AA detachments, reduced to three by the end of 1943.

What can be seen today?

All along the west coast of Jutland are considerable numbers of reinforced concrete fortifications, some of them have been restored and have become museums. These include:

- *Stellung Tirpitz* (see p147) The building of this bunker at Blåvand began in 1944 and it was designed to house a 38cm naval gun. The German surrender came before it was completed and postwar attempts to demolish it failed. The museum was opened on 1 June 1991.
- *Museums Center, Hanstholm* (see p151) Immediately after the German invasion in 1940, the building of Fortress Hanstholm began, naval artillery positions being established to protect supply routes to Norway and the unfinished Hanstholm Harbour, while flak batteries protected the approach to Alborg air base. Four SKS/34 38cm naval guns were installed in individual casemates, each with a crew of 90 men. The battery became operational in September 1941. The Hanstholm battery was moved to its present location beginning in 1942 and completed in June 1944. The guns were never to fire in their new casemates. The civilian population was evacuated in 1942 and the area became a major defensive position, stretching from Agger to Svinkov. In the autumn of 1945 the first civilians returned, but it was not until 1959 that the fortification was declared free of mines.
- *Bunker Museum Hirtshals* (p155) The museum consists of 54 excavated bunkers with many gun, mortar and MG emplacements, radar and searchlight installations.
- *Frederikshavn Batterie Süd* (p157) Today known as Bangsbo Fort, the battery boasted four 15cm naval guns from the *Nils Juel* with optical fire control and radar support, and Flak protection with batteries of various AA weapons from 20mm to 10.5cm. There are more than 50 bunkers of various types.
- *Frederikshavn Batterie Nord* Part of the German defensive system around this important harbour, an exhibition is housed in the original fire control bunker and an emplacement complete with 10.5cm gun has been re-established.

There are—unsurprisingly—not many signs of the Atlantic Wall left on the German coast. A few bunkers can still be found in some areas—some have even been turned into weekend seaside chalets—but in general terms, and for obvious reasons, the wall is no more.

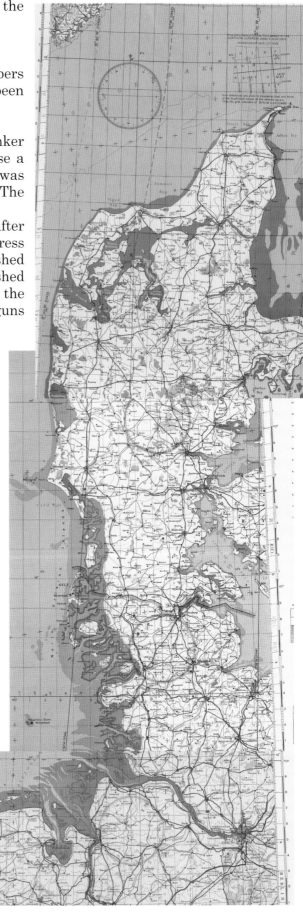

3

4

The Wadden Sea Islands and Blåvand

1 *The Wadden Sea islands off the southwest coast of Denmark were heavily fortified. They protected Esbjerg, the major west Jutland port that was seen as an inviting target for an Allied invasion. This L485 for a Mammut radar is on Rømø—by the end of the war, the island had the most advanced radar positions in Denmark. One of them was used to locate the point of impact of the V-2 bombs in England.* Elgaard/WikiCommons/ CC BY-SA 4.0

2 *Fanø, the northernmost Wadden Sea island, and Esbjerg were the most fortified areas in Denmark with some 1,200–1,300 bunkers. There were five coast artillery positions on Fanø, and a number of heavy (10.5cm) Flak emplacements.* Saxo/WikiCommons

3 *The famous* Stellung Tirpitz *at Blåvand was a battery built in the last months of the war but never finished. Both S561 emplacements for double 38cm turrets were unfinished. One of them is now a museum, part of the Varde City Museum.* KLM

4 and Main photo *StpGr Blåvand, another defender of Esbjerg, included HKB 7./180 situated around the lighthouse. It employed four 10.5cm K331(f) guns. This is a V174 radar bunker that could be used in conjunction with, for example, the FuMO 214 Giant Würzburg (Sea).* KLM; Matthias Süßen/ WikiCommons

5 *Bunkers as art. This is* Bunker/Mule (1995) *by Bill Woodrow, a permanent installation along the beach at Blåvand-Oksby. The F-Stand flanking MG casemates are part of 1. Stellung Blåvand -Skallingen. There are over 500 Heer F-stands—bunkers built outside the Regelbau programme.* Bill Woodrow

Søndervig

Left: *In the distance HKB 5./180's 636 looms. The sea has damaged it and the other bunkers in recent years. StPGr Søndervig included coastal battery HKB 5./180 of four 10.5cm K331(f) guns at Kryle and Luftwaffe StP Ringelnatter to the south.* KLM

Below Left: *Before the construction of concrete bunkers, the occupying Germans either took over the existing structures or set up their batteries in the open. This photo is from 1940.* Bundesarchiv, Bild 101I-755-0164-12/Bieling/CC-BY-SA 3.0

Main photo: 1 *636,* **2** *Tobruk once part of* **3**, **3** *671,* **4** *R501.* Ashley Jenkins

Opposite, Inset: *The base of a FuSE-65 Giant Würzburg on the beach at Kryle.* KLM

Defences of Limfjord

Right: *North of Søndervig at Husby this 680 casemate for a flanking 7.5cm PaK 40 is today washed by the North Sea. There are many such flanking casemates along the sandy beaches of Denmark's west coast.* KLM

Below Right: *StPGr Thyborøn protected the entrance to Limfjord. One of the Thyborøn strongpoints was StP HKB 4./180, whose main armament was four French 10.5cm guns. This is the 636 command post. Note the interesting attempt to camouflage the bunker as a farmhouse. During WW2 more than 100 bunkers were built in the area.* KLM

Below: *The northern side of the fjord was protected by StP Agger-Dorf. This 600 is on the beach.* KLM

Opposite:

1 The north of Denmark was heavily defended, particularly at Hanstholm (then called VB Hansted) and Vigsø. Strategically vital, guns from here controlled the southern section of the Skagerrak and—paired with those at Batterie Vara in Kristiansand, Norway—entry into the Baltic.

2 Taken just after the war, this shows one of the big guns at Hanstholm. There were four 38cm SK C/34 guns intended for Gneisenau installed here. Lklundin/WikiCommons/ CC BY-SA 4.0

Hanstholm

3 *Hanstholm was one of the largest Atlantic Wall sites with an infantry Stützpunkt, no fewer than four AA batteries with 10.5cm and 7.5cm guns and two artillery batteries: Hanstholm I, StP 1./MAA118, a battery armed with four 17cm guns in M270 casemates, and 38cm Hanstholm II battery, StP 2./MAA118. Four SK C/34 guns intended for the Gneisenau gave the battery the firepower to protect the southern side of the Skagerrak. Although they were scrapped in the early 1950s, the emplacements are still there now part of an impressive museum. Outside the museum are three weapons: a barrel for one of the 38cm guns (nearest the camera), a 15cm turret and in the distance a Russian 122mm.* KLM

4 *In the dunes to the west is Hanstholm I battery.* KLM

5 *The S100 Leitstand for Hanstholm II.* Petr Podebradsky

Vigsø

This Page and Opposite, Below:
In 1941 the Germans started building the complex at Vigsø to protect Hanstholm's eastern flank. As identified below, there were numerous casemates (671) and other bunkers—including a 636 fire control, Flak and personnel bunkers—built from 1942. Today the sea has encroached onto the site. KLM; Petr Podebradsky (p153)

Bulbjerg

Left and Below: *An infantry strong-point was set up in Bulbjerg in 1942. Concrete bunkers started to appear in 1943. Here (**Below**) an 622 personnel shelter and (**Left**) the S449 measuring position used in conjunction with the main fire-control for 2/MAA18.* www.bulbjerg.com; KLM (Below)

Løkken

This Page: *The next main strong-point along the coast was StPGr Løkken, a key position in the defence of the beaches of Jammerbugten Bay, seen as a location ripe for invasion. Løkken was heavily defended with batteries to north (Stp Königstein) and south of the town (Sperr-batterie Lökken-Süd) plus a sizeable infantry Stützpunkt. There were also radar sites to north (Luftwaffe) and south (Kriegsmarine). The southern naval coastal battery had 15cm guns taken from the Danish coastal defence ship Niels Juel. As can be seen from the photographs, the beach today is littered with lots of bunkers including this M272 (**Right**) a fine M162 fire control (**Below**). KLM (all)*

Hirtshals

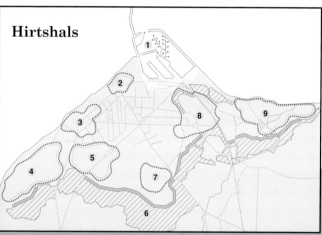

The defence of Hirtshals followed the same pattern as many other locations in Denmark. Strategically placed on the Skagerrak, in 1941 10.5cm coastal batteries were set up to the south and north of the port under 10./ and 9./HKAR 180 respectively. Later, from 1942, bunkers were built and the StPGr ended the war as shown in the plan (**Above**), where **1** is the harbour; **2** WN Bodensee; **3** WN Watzmann; **4** 10th Battery 'Semmering'; **5** Infantry StP Grossglockner; **6** Minefield; **7** Infantry StP Brenner; **8** Infantry StP Zillertal; **9** 9th Battery 'Wetterstein.' There are four 671 gun bunkers and four open emplacements for 10.5cm guns in the southern battery which had two L409A AA bunkers and radar for air and sea control. This is where Bunker Museum Hirtshals is located, Denmark's only excavated and complete German installation. Some 54 bunkers have been excavated. Those shown here are: **A** Fl277 emplacement for a 150cm searchlight from the southern battery; **B** 645 kitchen bunker; **C** a 636 HKB command post; **D** back to the southern battery—a 501 and the battery 636 (right). www.bunkerpictures.nl (A, B, C); Tomasz Sienicki/WikiCommons/CC BY 3.0 (D)

Skagen

This Page: At the very tip of Denmark, StPGr Skagen saw building by all three German services: infantry StP Hamburg; Luftwaffe sites; and Kriegsmarine coastal battery Lübeck (**Below** at **A**). MKB 2./509 Lübeck had four 12cm 390/1 (r) 'Pushka' guns housed in M272 casemates, various Flak bunkers, ammunition bunkers, personnel shelters and an M162a fire control post. Today, erosion means that many of these bunkers sit on the beach. In fact many of StP Hamburg's bunkers are now covered by sand, but one that isn't is the 638 Sanitätsunterstand (aid station) at **1**. It houses the Skagen Bunker Museum. Hamburg had five 622s, a 633 emplacement for an M19 mortar, a 506 casemate for an 4.7cm anti-tank gun, two L409s for air defence, and many others. There was a significant Luftwaffe presence: the first had but two bunkers—a 622 twin group bunker (**2** and **3**) and a V174 radar bunker for a FuMG Seetakt, used to spot ships. The V174 is so badly destroyed that it is very hard to make out. Also within the infantry StP is a Luftwaffe Fernsuchanlage (long-distance search facility) with an L480 Wassermann S (heavy) radar. Across the peninsula is Luftwaffe StP Schakal, with a number of radars. South of the town of Skagen, the Leebstellung stretched anti-tank defences across the peninsula. Matthias Schalk/WikiCommons/CC BY-SA 3.0; Zairon/WikiCommons/CC BY-SA 3.0; KLM

Frederikshavn

This Page: *VB Frederikshavn saw activity from the early days of the German occupation. In 1940 the Kriegsmarine set up a coastal battery and an AA battery in the hills at Pikkerbakken. Later there were strongpoints at the harbour, airfield and the town, including radar sites and AA batteries. Today, the Bangsbo Fort Museum has preserved 70 bunkers including three of the coastal battery's original 15cm guns—as at Løkken taken from Niels Juel—in their M272 casemates (**Above**); a number of 622s including this one (**Left**) and an M162a Leitstand (**Below**). In both north and south there were also AA batteries equipped with 10.5cm FlaK guns. KLM; Västgöten/Wiki-Commons (Left and Below)*

6 NORWAY

Passage leading to the bunker of the Norwegian wartime leader Vidkun Quisling. His hated collaboration with Nazi Germany led to his surname becoming synonymous with betrayal. The Times used it first and Winston Churchill picked it up: 'A vile race of Quislings—to use a new word which will carry the scorn of mankind down the centuries—is hired to fawn upon the conqueror, to collaborate in his designs and to enforce his rule upon their fellow countrymen while groveling low themselves.' Quisling and his Nasjonal Samling party ran Norway 1942–45. He was executed by firing squad in Oslo on 24 October 1945. Gulosten/WikiCommons/CC BY-SA 4.0

The German invasion of Norway took place the month before Fall Gelb, the offensive in the Low Countries. Although taken by surprise when the attack came on 8–9 April 1940, the sinking of the *Blücher*, carrying invasion troops, by the guns of Oscarsborg Fortress gave the Norwegian royal family enough time to escape.

After the withdrawal of the Allied forces two months later and the Norwegian capitulation, the Germans occupation began. It would be five hard years before Norway was free. The civil administration under Reichskommissar Josef Terboven (until his suicide in 1945), assisted by Vidkun Quisling and his *Nasjonal Samling* party, ensured supply to Germany of the raw materials their industry needed, confiscating over 50 percent of Norwegian output. In the face of organised resistance—and fear of Allied invasion—the German garrison was sizeable, with around one German soldier for every ten Norwegians. The Army of Occupation was commanded from 1940 until December 1944 by Generaloberst Nikolaus von Falkenhorst, with Generalleutnant Rudolf Bamler as his chief of staff (1942–February 1944) who then handed over to Generalmajor Eugen Theilacker. Subordinate formations in June 1944 were XXXIII, LXX and LXXI Armeekorps with 89th Inf Div (the 'Horseshoe' Division) in reserve. This division had been created in 1944 from personnel in the reinforced regiments of the Replacement Army and trained in Norway March–June 1944, returning to central Europe about the time of the Normandy invasion. It was ordered first to the Rouen–Le Havre area, then on to Normandy in late June where it suffered heavy casualties. Its place as Army Group Reserve was taken by the Norway Panzer Brigade.

In October 1944 the Russian advance through Finland finally reached Norway, forcing the Germans to retreat south. Hitler agreed the troops should pull back and a scorched earth retreat left Finnmark burning as the Red Army advanced. On 25 October a Norwegian force set sail for Murmansk from Britain to join the Soviet forces now entering Northern Norway. Commanded by Oberst A. D. Dahl they arrived on Norwegian soil on 10 November, but it would take into April before Finnmark was completely freed. German forces in Norway capitulated soon after.

The protection of Norway was given top priority by the Germans from the start because it was difficult to bring in reinforcements and there were such a large number of potential landing sites and ports to defend. The occupation forces were only able to protect properly the entrances to the fjords and the islands off the coast. The interior coasts of the fjords were thinly defended, but strongpoints protected the military bases and main access routes into the interior. Designated as the main defensive areas were Narvik, Lofoten Islands, Langøy, Tromsø, Bodø, Mo, Vega, Rorvik, Trondheim, Kristiansund, Alesund, Solund, Bergen, Stavanger, Flekkefjord, Kristiansand, Arendal, Tønsberg and Oslo. The three most important were Narvik, Bergen and Trondheim, not just because of its submarine pens but also the Nordstern project (see p174).

There were some 225 artillery batteries of all types around the coast, around 1,000 heavy and medium guns—over 40 of which were 24cm or larger in calibre. Good examples of these super-heavies were Battery Trondenes near Narvik, armed with four 40.6cm naval guns in turrets, and the 28cm triple-gun turret at Fort Austrått (Ørlandet, east of Trondheim), guarding the far reaches of Trondheim Fjord. This turret was originally the stern gun turret of the German battleship *Gneisenau*. After seeing action during the early part of the war, the *Gneisenau* was badly damaged in February 1942, and its guns taken ashore. 'A' turret's guns were set up individually at the Hook of Holland. The undamaged 'B' turret was mounted in a mountain installation at Fjell on the island of Sotra, west of Bergen; the 'C' turret came to Austrått. Before it was emplaced the necessary shafts and tunnels had to be blasted out of the mountain and comprehensive concrete work carried out. The building work was done by 300–400 Serbian POWs, who lived in terrible conditions and were roughly treated. Many Serbs died during the work which began in 1942 and was completed the following year. In spring 1945 the guns became part of the Trondelag coastal artillery brigade, later called Fort Austrått.

In addition to the gun batteries there were 15 torpedo batteries of various sizes (one to four tubes) protected by concrete bunkers.

What can be seen today?

Unlike Denmark, the fortifications and defensive positions in Norway were solidly built on and into rock, so erosion has proved less significant and many of the fortifications have survived in situ to the present day.

The jewels in the crown must be the big gun museums at the batteries mentioned earlier: Battery Trondenes, Fortress Fjell and Fort Austrått. The latter ended its military use in 1968, and in 1990 the Norwegian Defence Department funded restoration work. Once this had been completed, the battery was handed over to the municipality of Orland as a tourist attraction and opened to the public in May 1992.

Oscarsborg Fortress in Oslofjord—with the battery that sank the *Blücher*—is also a significant location. Kristiansand Kanonmuseum has the only remaining WW2 38cm naval gun. The complex was operational by 1943 and named Batterie Vara (see p165). Together with the gun at Hanstholm, across the Skagerrak in Denmark (see pp151), its main task was to protect German supply lines and deny Allied forces access to the Baltic. Another preserved battery near Kristiansand is Ny-Hellesund Coastal Fort—which includes two K331(f) guns in 671 bunkers, one in an open emplacement, and other weapons.

Other museum locations include Kvalik Fort, which was sited to control Omsundet and the entrance to Freifjorden and Vinjefjorden. As well as bunkers its weapons include a 12cm K370(b) and 15cm SKL/45. Tellevik Kystfort (Åsane, Bergen) has many surviving bunkers and several guns on outdoor display—including K331(f), K332(f) and a 10.5cm SK C/32.

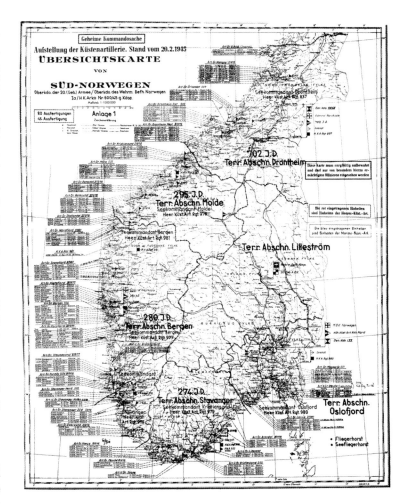

Top: *The German military regions and coastal batteries in southern Norway as of 20 February 1945.*

Above: L–R, *Vidkun Quisling, Heinrich Himmler, Josef Terboven—the German Reichskommissar in Norway—and Nikolaus von Falkenhorst seated in front of officers of the Waffen-SS, Heer and Luftwaffe in 1941. Bundesarchiv, Bild 101III-Moebius-029-12/Möbius/CC-BY-SA 3.0*

(see p162)

Batteries around Oslo

1 MKB 2./Marine-ersatzabteilung
   (5./501) Oscarsborg
2 MKB 1./501 Dröbak
3 HKB 7./980 Kjököen
4 HKB 6./980 Torgauten
5 MKB 2./501 Rauöy (see p162)
6 HKB 8./980 Kongshavn
7 MKB 3./501 Bolärne (see p162)
8 MKB 6./501 Nötteröy (see p162)
9 MKB 4./501 Toraas
10 Railwayartillery-batterie 689

1a

1b

3

4

Oslo

Opposite: *1942 map of Oslo area identfiying the German batteries in the area. The guns of Oscarsborg Fortress (**1**) in Oslofjord, under command of Oberst Birger Eriksen, were instrumental in the sinking of the German heavy cruiser Blücher on 9 April 1940. The fortress's armament—a TT battery and three 28cm calibre guns manufactured by Krupp (one shown at **1a**)—performed perfectly even though handled by a partly green crew. The battle involved a number of the Norwegian batteries. First, the battery on Rauøy (**5**) spotted the convoy and fired warning shots. When the Germans did not respond, it fired more shots but missed. The next battery to engage was that of Bolærne (**6**), which also fired a warning shot. Blücher kept going to reach Oslo by dawn, passing close by Oscarsborg whose 28cm guns hit the Blücher twice before 533mm torpedoes launched from North Kaholmen Island finished the job. Around 700 Germans perished when Blücher capsized and sank (**Above Left** and **Left**). Here, (**1b**) Oscarsborg fortress from the southwest and above. KEBman/WikiCommons (1a)*

Opposite, 3: *HKB 7./980 Kjököen was built between April and May 1941 with four 10cm K17/04 guns. In 1943, two 88mm Flak pieces were added. This is the command bunker. Tommy Gildseth via WikiCommons*

Opposite, 4 and Left: *HKB 6./980 Torgauten was also built April–May 1941 with the same weapons. In September 1944, two 10.5cm K331(f) guns were added at Mörvika. The battery today is a museum. Area1970/WikiCommons (both)*

Above: *The last operational fort in Oslofjord, Bolaerne was involved in the fight with the Blücher. During the occupation MKB 3./501 Bolärne (note the difference between Norwegian and German spellings) was equipped with four 15cm L/50 Bofors guns. Tommy Gildseth via WikiCommons*

Right: *Construction of MKB 6./501 Nötteröy started in March 1944 but it remained unfinished at the end of the war, although two 38cm KM36/35(f) naval guns had been installed. As an interesting continuation, after the war the guns were returned to France in exchange for 38cm SK C/34s (as employed in MKB Vara) which had been removed from Batterie Todt. The battery was scrapped in the 1950s. WikiCommons/Lars Åge Kamfjord/ CC-BY-SA 3.0*

Below Right: *One of the two remaining 15cm SK C/28 guns of Fort Rauøy, one of the batteries involved in the battle with the Blücher. The guns were installed in 1963 and casemated in 1966. During the war the Germans had a naval artillery school there and four 15cm SK L/45s. Tommy Gildseth via WikiCommons*

South Norway

Left: *The 636 of HKB 34./979 Flostaöen at Kalvøysund, part of ArGr Arendal, was a large complex equipped originally with four 10.5cm K332(f) guns. These were replaced in August 1944 with K331(f) guns.*KEN/WikiCommons

Below and Bottom Left: *Fort Folehavna lies at the tip of Sandefjord east of Larvik. Under German control it was named Vestero and housed HKB 5./980 Vesterøen, part of ArGr Larvik, equipped with four 12cm K370(b) guns. Illustrated are a Flak position (**Below Left**) and the observation bunker (**Bottom**).*Tommy Gildseth via WikiCommons; Bundesarchiv, Bild 101I-113-0003-15/Volgger/ CC-BY-SA 3.0

Above: *Formed in 1941, Den Norske Legion—the Norwegian unit of the SS—saw volunteers enlist expecting to fight under Norwegian officers in Finland against the Russians. Instead, they fought under Germans in Russia mainly around Leningrad. The legion was disbanded in March 1943, and the few who wanted to keep fighting joined 11th SS Volunteer Panzergrenadier Division Nordland.*

163

Right: *Fort Justøya was home to HKB 31./979 Justöen, part of ArUGr Lillesand, four 10.5cm K332(f) guns and two Flak positions, several bunkers, a network of tunnels and this 636.* Tommy Gildseth via WikiCommons

Below: *HKB 21./979 Ny-Hellesund was located on the island of Askøya, part of ArUGr Sögne. Equipped with four 10.5cm K331(f) Schneider guns—one of them shown in its 671 casemate—Batterie 21./979 deployed there in March 1943. The complex, interconnected by tunnels, with many other bunkers including a 636 fire control and a Flak position, had been built by 200 Russian PoWs.* kalev kevad/ WikiCommons

Today's Fort Møvik was called Batterie Vara (MAB 6./502 Vara) by the Germans. It was heavily armed with four 38cm SK C/34 guns with a range of 42,000m (26 miles), one in a turret (**Above and Below**) and the others on S169 emplacements (**Top**) which were dismantled during the 1960s. Part of ArGr Kristiansand, it had a Flak unit (Batterie 303./III with four 88mm Flak 37s) and a 15cm SK L/45 gun to fire starshells located at Randöya. The guns were tasked with guarding the Skagerrak in conjunction with their sister battery at Hanstholm in Denmark, 116km across the strait. It was one of seven coastal and five Flak batteries defending Kristiansand. Petr Podebradsky (Top and Above); Bundesarchiv, Bild 101I-116-0346-25/Lange/CC-BY-SA 3.0 (Right); Bundesarchiv, Bild 101I-113-0010-17/Rehor, Willy/CC-BY-SA 3.0 (Below)

Left: *CP of HKB 16./981 Risnes. Equipped with four 10.5cm K332(f)s and, from 1942, two 88mm Flak, it came under ArGr Sognefjord. Together with 14./ and 15./981, MAA504/7 and Torpedobatterie Rutledal it was tasked with protecting the entrance to Sognesjøen and Sognefjord.* Jeblad/WikiCommons/CC BY-SA 3.0 (both)

Below Left: *Contemporary map showing Randaberg (**1**), Stavanger (**2**), Brusand (**3**) and Batterie Vara (**4**; see p165). Randaberg was the HQ for Seekommandant Stavanger (regional coastal commander)and Artilleriekommandeur Stavanger (regional artillery commander), HKAR 978.*

Below: *'Hitler's teeth'—ATk defences built by local labour on Jæren to hinder an Allied attack along Route 44 at Brusand in Hå (**3**).* Jarle Vines/WikiCommons/ CC BY 3.0

Opposite, Above: *HKB 34./977 Gavlen was part of ArGr Hjeltefjord. It was armed with four 10.5cm K332(f)s situated on the headland above Torpedobatterie Hjelte with its three 533mm TTs completed in 1944. Guarding the approaches to the battery were two LT35 turrets each armed with a 37mm gun.* Petr Podebadsky

Opposite, Centre Left: *Fort Kvarven was built on high ground to defend Bergen harbour. In 1940 the battery knocked out the German Bremen and Carl Peters and damaged the battleship Königsberg. Under German occupation it housed MKB 1./ and 2./504 armed with three 21cm L/45 St Chamond guns and three 24cm St Chamond respectively. It is a museum today.* Haakon Nilsen/WikiCommons

Bergen

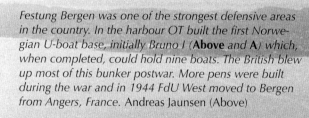

Festung Bergen was one of the strongest defensive areas in the country. In the harbour OT built the first Norwegian U-boat base, initially Bruno I (**Above** and **A**) which, when completed, could hold nine boats. The British blew up most of this bunker postwar. More pens were built during the war and in 1944 FdU West moved to Bergen from Angers, France. Andreas Jaunsen (Above)

This Page: *MKB 11./504 Fjell is a large 185-acre complex on a high point of Sotra island, on the approaches to Bergen. Its main armanant was the 'B' turret of the Gneisenau, with three 28cm SK C/34 guns—very similar to the turrets of the 28cm-armed Deutschland (seen* **Right** *via NARA). The turret isn't there any more—as can be seen* **Below Right**. *It was scrapped in 1968 when the Norwegian National Defence used the site first as a coastal defence and then as a radar station. They left in 2004 and the site has become a museum and the emplacement houses a café. The extensive site was defended by bunkers housing anti-tank guns, flame-throwers, machine guns, mortars, and six Fl242 2cm Flak positions.* Andreas Sandberg/WikiCommons/ CC BY-SA 3.0

Below: *This photo shows (***A***) a Type 633 M19 mortar bunker which is attached to the tunnel system around the gunshaft. The steel cover at* **B** *is from a later date. On the horizon (***C***) the S446 Leitstand.* SinWin/Wiki-Commons/CC BY-SA 3.0

Kristiansund

This Page: *Batterie HKB 17./976 Bud came under ArGr Möre. Around 200km west of Kristiansund, construction of the battery —six 15.5cm K416(f) guns (A)— began in April 1941 and continued for about two years, linking some of the bunkers through an underground tunnel system. Now a museum, highlights include an original 150cm FuMO 3 Flakscheinwerfer (searchlight) which stands in front of the museum (B) and a 636 fire-control bunker (C).* Ernst Vikne/WikiCommons/CC BY-SA 2.0; Halvard Hatlen/WikiCommons/CC-BY-SA-2.5; Cato Edvardsen/WikiCommons/CC-BY-SA-2.5

169

Torpedo launchers

As well as a range of coastal artillery batteries Norway had a number of fixed, land-based torpedo batteries. Some of these—such as that at Oscasborg that helped sink the Blücher—were originally Norwegian; others were emplaced by the Germans. Some launched their torpedoes underwater; others from the shoreline. Towards the end of the war the Germans developed the Spinne (Spider), a torpedo electrically controlled from the shore by a cable, which had a range of 6,000yd and a speed of 30kts, but the war was over before it could see use.

1 *Torpedobatterie Hasselvik on Hysneståa was established in April 1940 and made use of the rear topedo tubes (4 x 53cm) from the destroyer* Paul Jacobi. *Part of ArGr Drontheim-ost, (MAA506), it was companion to Torpedobatterie Hammbaara whose tubes came from destroyer* Theodor Riedl *in June 1940.* Bundesarchiv, Bild 101I-116-0336-05/Ebert/CC-BY-SA 3.0

2 *Torpedobatterie Sørviknes replaced Hasselvik (which was then closed), part of a 1943 building program to strengthen Trondheim's defenses.* Tommy Gildseth

3 *Torpedobatterie Julholmen was one of two such in ArGr Möre (MAA505)—the other was Otterøy-Süd—both had two 45cm TTs (upgraded in July 1944 with 52cm TTs).* Tommy Gildseth

4 *Torpedobatterie Nordlandet was part of ArGr Kristiansund and ready for action in December 1944, although it saw no use during the war.* Tommy Gildseth

Trondheim

Above Left: *Attacked on 9 April 1940, Hysnes Fort surrendered that afternoon after having damaged the* Theodor Riedel. *The Germans turned it into a coastal battery—MKB Hysnes 2./506. Today, it's a museum.* Tommy Gildseth

Left: *HKB 5./981 Floröy in Sogn og Fjordane was equipped with six 15.5cm Schneider Model 1917 field guns—identified as K416(f) in German service, one of which is in situ today.* Rakein-thecache

Befitting its importance to the Germans, Trondheim—or Drontheim as it is in German—is surrounded by batteries (see map **Opposite, Bottom**). The most significant, perhaps, is MKB 4./507 Örlandet—today's Fort Austrått—dominated by the unusual sight of a three-gun battleship turret. When Gneisenau was seriously damaged in 1942, its three turrets were parcelled out: one to Austrått, one to Fortress Fjell on Sotra outside Bergen (see p168) and the third, the one damaged in an air raid, saw its guns individually casemated in S412 bunkers as part of Battery Rozenburg at the Hoek van Holland (see p126). Of the nine 28.3cm guns, only those at Austrått remain, atop a five-storey, 15m-deep installation fitted into a hole hewed from the rock which also housed all the facilities needed to maintain and fight with the turret. It was constructed by Yugoslav PoWs, many of whom died because of the extreme working conditions. Today it is an excellent museum.

Above Right: StP Mitte included the command bunker (now a museum) for ArGr Drontheim West, an SK 117a that connects to a Tobruk on which—today—sits a Czech PzKpfw38(t) turret. Petr Podebradsky

Right, Below Right and Bottom: Today the rangefinder for the battery is near the Gneisenau turret (**Right**). During the war it sat on a ring atop the S446 fire-control bunker (**Below Right**) on the summit of a hill overlooking the fjord. Petr Podebradsky (all)

Below: Close defence included an 631 4.7cm PaK casemate which has a restored weapon. www.bunkerpictures.nl

Bottom: Gneisenau's 'C'—Caesar—turret at Fort Austrått. Petr Podebradsky

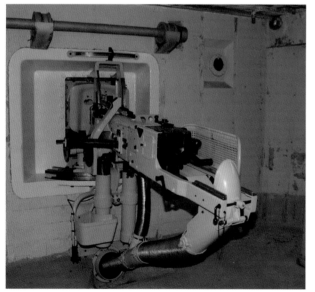

Trondheim

The external defences of Trondheim included these main locations:

A MKB 3./506 Lökhaug
   (4 x 15cm SKL/45)
B HKB 19./975 Storfosen
   (6 x 15cm K403(j))
C HKB 16./975 Hovde
   (5 x 10.5cm K335(h))
D MKB 1./507 Husöen
   (3 x 28cm SKL/45)
E HKB 18./975 Hoö
   (4 x 10.5cm K331(f))
F MKB 4./507 Örlandet
   (Fort Austrått; 3 x 28cm SK C/34)
G HKB 17./975 Selnes
H MKB 1./506 Brettingen
   (as above)
I MKB 2./506 Hysnes
   (2 x 21cm L/45 Armstrong guns; 2 x 15cm L/47.5 Armstrongs)
J Torpedobatterie Hasselvik
K MKB 5./506 Stördal
   (3 x 10cm SK C/32)
L Fort Hambaara (MKB 4./506 Hambaara—3 x 12cm L/44 Armstrong guns; Torpedobatterie Hammbaara)
M HKB 21./975 Hevnskjöl-Süd (6 x 21 cm Mrs(t) mortars); HKB 23./975 Hevskjöl-Nord (4 x 15.5cm K416(f))
N HKB 27./975 Melland-Ost
   (4 x 10.5cm K331(f))
O HKB 22./975 Melland-West (4 x 15cm K16 guns)

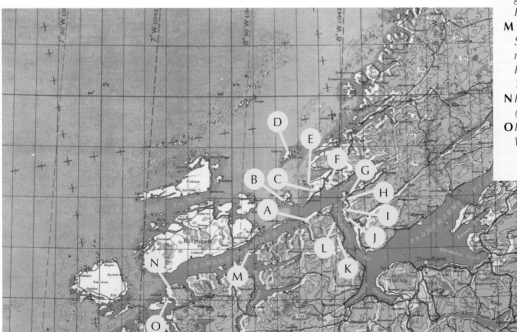

Left and Below Left: *Trondheim was not just important for its submarine base, but as the site for a new city, Nordstern (North Star), that Hitler planned to build locally. Intended for for 250,000–300,000 inhabitants, work started on the project in 1943 with the creation at Øysand of a PoW camp for labour and a reserve airstrip. The deteriorating war situation ended the plan in 1944. By then, Trondheim had become the largest German naval base in northern Europe, housing the 13th U-boat flotilla. The Germans built one U-boat bunker, Dora I, in 1941–43 and started Dora II, but only Dora I had been completed by the end of the war. It had five pens and could cater for 16 U-boats.* USAF

Opposite, Top: *Note Dora I at* **A**. USAF

Opposite, Centre Left: *On 7 December 2009, a sign that probably hung at Stiftsgården, the office of Trondheim's Reich Commissariat, was recovered from the River Nid by a team of marine archeologists from NTNU University Museum.* MediaWizard/WikiCommons

Opposite, Centre Right: *Captured German U-boats—a Type VII and a Type IX—outside their pen, 19 May 1945.*

Below: *Dora I now serves as an archive centre for municipal, university library and museums.* University library at Norwegian University of Science and Technology via WikiCommons

Nordland
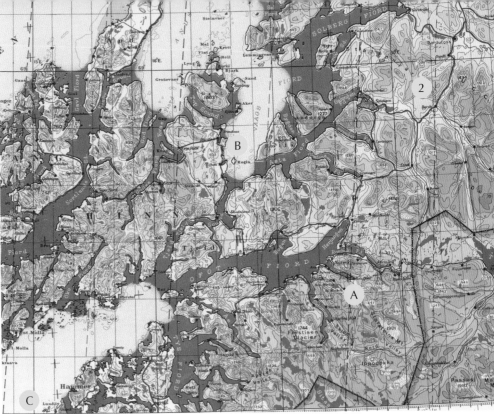

1 *MKB 4./516 Dietl was armed with three huge 40.6cm SK C/34 guns with a range of 56,000m (35 miles) housed in S384 casemates. The guns of Batterie Dietl were ready by August. This is the S100 Leitstand looking out from the island of Engeløya over the Vestfjord.* Petr Podebradsky

2 *Narvik (A) and its two big-gun batteries:* **B** *Batterie Trondenes and* **C** *Batterie Dietl.*

3 *MKB 5/511 Trondenes was armed with four 40.6cm SK C/34 guns. Three of the guns were ready for action in May 1943; the last in August. As elsewhere in Norway, the heavy labour at Trondenes was carried out by Russian PoWs, who were treated very poorly.* Petr Podebradsky

4 *The Germans bombed Bodø on 27 May 1940 causing huge destruction to the town. Their ground forces arrived on 1 June. During the war many defences were built (see the excellent www.thomaslillevoll.net for details), often using Russian PoWs many of whom died before the Red Army liberated the area on 9 May 1945. Here, in late autumn 1943 soldiers move a heavy gun at HKB 4./974 Straumöy-Süd.* Bundesarchiv, Bild 101I-118-0379-20 / Ebert / CC-BY-SA

5 *Another battery—MKB 6./510 Arnøy—was employed to defend the waters around Bodø. It had four 15cm SKL/45 gun turrets, three of which are still in situ, along with two 622 personnel bunkers and a three-level M157 fire control post.* Petr Podebradsky

6 *Batterie HKB 16./974 Grönsviken was built at Stokkvågen by Russian and Polish labourers, whose story is covered in the barracks, today a museum. Armed with four 155mm K416(f) guns, it was one of ten coastal batteries that made up the ArGr Sandnessjöen whose task was to defend the crucial road and rail corridor from south to northern Norway—the supply route to the Finnmark front and the route back for iron destined* for Germany. This is the SK Leitstand. Ingeeiliv/WikiCommons/ CC BY-SA 3.0

7 *Further south, Batterie HKB 32./974 Brönnöysund-nord was one of three batteries that made up Artillery Group Brönnöysund. Ready in June 1941, it was armed with four 15.5cm K416(b) guns, one of which is preserved.* Petr Podebradsky

8 *South of Brönnöysund and north of Trondheim ArGr Namsos included Batterie HKB 2./975 Utvorden Süd. Armed with six 15.5cm 416(f) guns and was ready for action in June 1942. There were seven batteries in the group and a torpedo battery, MAA506, with four 533mm (21in) TTs (h). There were 18 such torpedo batteries in Norway. This the Vf Leitstand.* Petr Podebradsky

ARMS FOR RUSSIA . . . A great convoy of British ships escorted by Soviet fighter planes sails into Murmansk harbour with vital supplies for the Red Army.

Finnmark

This page: *In the far north of Norway, up in the Arctic Circle, the country borders on Russia. The town of Vardø on the island of Vardøya is north of Kirkenes and less than 200km from Murmansk. The Russian port welcomed 78 Allied Lend-Lease convoys that braved the weather, the coastal guns and naval forces in the Barents Sea to maintain a lifeline to the USSR.* Crown Copyright/WikiCommons

Above and Below: *There were two HKBs on Vardøya—1./448 Vardö-Renösund (***1** *and* Leitstand **Above***) had four 10.5cm K331(f) guns, and 5./448 Vardö-Bussesund had three 21cm Mrs18s. Both were demolished and evacuated in October 1944. The island had a fort as early as 1306. Vardøhus Fortress (***2***) was extensively renovated in the 18th century and was an active unit of the Norwegian Navy under the command of Naval District 3 in Tromsø at the start of the war. It saw action once during the invasion, on 4 June 1940 when attacked by a Luftwaffe bomber which limped away with a wounded navigator after being hit by ground fire. Occupied from 17 July, Vardøhus became a German barracks. In 1944, retreating from the Russians, the Germans burned Vardø*

leaving little standing. Jim Watson, Ontario, Canada

Opposite: *Wartime shots of German batteries in Finnmark.* **A and B** *Heavy Flak position of MKB 4./513 Vardö with 88mm Flak 37, later evacuated to MKB 3./516 Lödingen in October 1944 as the Russians advanced.* **C** *Camouflaged 28cm SKL/45 gun 'Scharnhorst' of MAB 3./513 Kiberg. It saw combat with the advancing Soviets and was also destroyed in October 1944;* **D** *Leitstand of MAB 4./517 Mestersand. This position had four 24cm SKL/40 guns and was also evacuated before the Soviets could take it in October 1944.* Bundesarchiv, Bild 101I-110-1699-23 (A); -21 (B); 1673-08 (C); 1694-34 (D)/Faßhauer/CC-BY-SA 3.0

7 ASSESSMENT

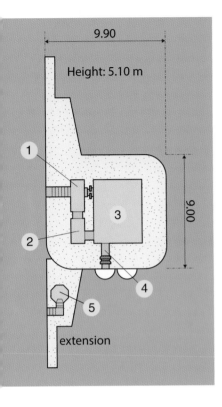

9.90

Height: 5.10 m

9.00

extension

Above: *The basic shelter was the 501 for ten men.*

Below: *This 501 can be found at Groede in Zeeland, part of the Breskens pocket. All photos on this spread* www.bunkerpictures.nl

How Good Were the Defences?

It is clear that the permanent reinforced concrete installations —bunkers— provided some protection from bombardment for the German infantry. From these positions close to the shoreline they were generally able to inflict considerable losses upon the enemy. The perfect example of this is the fighting on Omaha Beach which at one stage almost won the day. However, it is also true that the installations were vulnerable to fire from the sea, be it from naval vessels or close support landing craft—such as those carrying batteries of rockets—and it was the use of close-in support by destroyers that helped sustain the beleaguered US forces. Certainly the German losses, too, were considerable: the commander of 352nd Infantry Division said that on 6 June his division had lost one-fifth of its total infantry fighting strength.

Communications between all positions were a major weakness, frequently broken due to the telephone wires being damaged, irrespective of whether or not they were buried. This was a well-known hazard in defensive positions, but still occurred constantly and led to chaos, there being insufficient modern radios to replace/back up the telephone system, while specialist repairmen were always at a premium. This led to runners having to be used, causing delays and casualties.

Artillery, both coastal and field, generally did well initially, but was then badly affected by enemy air strikes, both on gun positions and, most importantly, on forward observers (the observers could be replaced but not their equipment). All types of artillery suffered from the fighter-bomber activity, which caused many casualties, especially to flak and anti-tank artillery. However, the worst problem of all was a general shortage of ammunition, compelling the defenders to use ammunition as sparingly as possible. This was exacerbated by the use of so many foreign weapons and the consequently huge range of calibres.

As part of their improvements to the Atlantic Wall, the Germans asked themselves whether the defences were good enough even before they were put to the ultimate test by the Normandy invasion. From autumn 1943, the Fortress Engineer staffs were required to report to Generalleutnant Rudolf Schmetzer, the inspector of western fortifications, who had been in the job since

15 August 1940, on the results of all enemy bombs released over the fortified defence systems in their areas; later, too, on the results of heavy naval guns firing at these emplacements. Schmetzer was ordered to Paris on 2 June 1944 to report on these investigations and the gist of his findings was produced in a written report which was translated and published for the US Army in 1947. The report was entitled: 'The effect of bombs and heavy naval guns on the fortified defence system of the Atlantic Wall.' Schmetzer had used not only the detailed reports which he had received, but he had also kept in touch with the OT, the chief naval fortress engineer staff and the staff at Luftflotte 3, and had carried out his own inspections of constructions with walls of reinforced-concrete 2m thick or over. Here are some examples of the results his report listed.

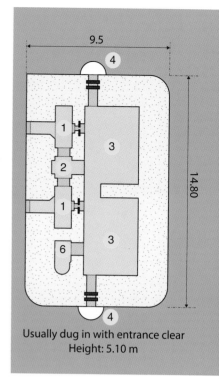

Usually dug in with entrance clear
Height: 5.10 m

Shelters

As far as Gruppe shelters were concerned (501/621 or 502/622 were the main types with totals of 1,553 and 1,728 respectively), he cites the case of a normal shelter made of 'faultless quality' reinforced concrete 2m thick, occupied by a sergeant and eight artillerymen, which received three direct hits during an air-raid. The first one hit one of the short walls (about 15sq m in size):

'At the explosion the whole construction rumbled and shook tremendously, so that bottles and other objects fell from the table. At the same time the electric lights went out, small bits of concrete fell down and the room was full of dust which made breathing somewhat difficult.

'A candle was lit. After a short time, when the dust had settled, minor damage could be observed, such as several very thin cracks in the wall and small pieces broken out of the supports carrying the iron roofgirders immediately beneath the roof.

'About 5–10 minutes later, the second direct hit landed on the unsupported part of the roof in distance only 50cm from the wall which had been hit before, producing the same results as the first direct hit. There were a few more cracks in the wall and they were slightly deeper, as were also the small pieces broken out from under the roof. To the men in the shelter; the damage appeared quite insignificant, now as before.

'After a further lapse of 10–15 minutes, the third direct hit landed, again on the roof, approximately 3m from where the second bomb had struck, about 1.5m from the short wall opposite and not much further from the long wall. The sergeant and three of the men, who were sitting with their backs towards the short wall which had been hit first of all, declared that everything had

Above: *The 502 sheltered 20 men.*

Below Left: *This 502 is from StPGr Schouwen, WN328H, Burgh-Haamstede.*

Below: *The successor to the 501 was the 3m-thick-walled 621. This one is at Moerdijk bridges.*

At Gatteville the casemates to take the artillery pieces had not been completed before they were captured. The field guns were still in open emplacements behind them. NARA

happened exactly as during the first two direct hits. They were convinced that the shelter had withstood the attack as before. It was only after the candle had again been lit and the dust had settled that they saw "The roof coming right down to the floor", and discovered four of their comrades dead under the debris, the fifth injured by a fragment of concrete, and a large gaping hole in the roof.'

Intensive examination was carried out and it was found that all three direct hits had been made by bombs of 500kg in weight. The building was so badly damaged that it could not be repaired. Despite this, the general feeling was that the shelter had not done badly, having survived two direct hits. Receiving three direct hits on a structure with an exposed surface of less than 10m x 15m was considered 'somewhat unusual'.

Casemates

Schmetzer cited the explosion of a heavy bomb (probably 250kg or heavier) which exploded in the air about 2m outside the open embrasure of a manned gun emplacement while the heavy armoured outer door at the rear was closed. While there were just a few deep scars on the brickwork caused by fragments, the blast had a devastating effect inside the casemate:

'The gun mount was damaged, although the barrel was still intact. The crew, 11 men, who had thrown themselves flat on the ground, were dead—burst lungs. One of them—presumably the only man not lying on the floor—had been hurled upwards and was hanging under the roof with the cloth of his jacket and trousers caught between the roof and the wall ... The armoured door had been torn out. Its lower wing was lying 30m to the rear of the structure and the upper wing 50m behind it. The gun embrasure remained fully serviceable, the gun ready to fire after its mount had been exchanged.'

Clearly the strong air pressure was to blame, especially as it 'rebounded' in the enclosed space. Whilst the chance of an airburst was infrequent, a hit on the concrete slab in front of the gun emplacement would have had much the same effect. The danger from the blast and fragmentation could only have been lessened had the large open embrasure been smaller. Also, the fact that the casemate was tightly closed in the rear enhanced the danger from blast. Perhaps this could have been lessened had the large gun door been open—but this would have presented a risk to the rear of the casemate from bomb splinters, which would have meant erecting an earth parapet, not too steeply sloped, in front of the open door.

Another case was that of a coastal battery, which had been under constant heavy air attack, resulting in penetration under two of its gun emplacements, followed by penetration from a naval armour-piercing shell of the largest calibre through one of them. It was an HKB of six 17cm or 20cm guns, northeast of the mouth of the Orne river on the Butte de Houlgate. The battery was comprised of six static guns—that is to say, guns on gun mounts on a concrete base—four of which were unprotected, whilst the fifth and sixth guns on the left wing of the site were in concrete emplacements, constructed in the usual manner. All shelters were of 2m thick reinforced-concrete. Schmetzer considered that this particular battery had been subjected to the heaviest bombing attacks: 'to a degree probably unequalled in the entire Atlantic Wall area'. When he inspected the battery on 24 June 1944, he found:

'The entire battery terrain was full of bomb craters, some of which had undoubtedly been caused by 1,000kg bombs. During the entire period, the total casualties in dead, wounded and sick amounted to only 25% (the battery had never been relieved), which must be attributed to some extent to the fact there was a sufficient number of shelters which were strong and that the air raid precautions system functioned extremely well. In spite of numerous direct hits, not one of the strong shelters for gun crews, ammunition, command and observation posts was put out of action or even seriously damaged.

'Of the four guns which were unprotected, one was still located, quite intact, in its old place. The barrel and gun mount did show several scratches caused by shell splinters, but the gun was only put out of action for two hours because of minor damage that was repaired then and there.

'The three remaining guns had all been slightly damaged (the exact dates of the particular damage were not known), to an extent which made it impossible for them to be repaired in their firing positions. They were dismantled and brought to rearward positions, where they were repaired in the Ordnance Depot. After two to four days at the most, they were again in working order and brought up to a new firing position. Although they fired frequently from there, they were neither spotted by the enemy nor hit by any more bombs, nor fired at—one of the reasons for the few serious losses suffered by the battery.

'On the other hand, both concrete gun emplacements were out of action. They had only been completed just before the invasion and showed signs of somewhat hasty construction. Their adaptation to the terrain, their protection by earth parapets and camouflage were faulty and the concrete did not appear to be completely flawless ... Each emplacement was badly damaged in several places by bombs which had penetrated beneath it and by close hits—large cracks, various big fragments broken out of the rear walls, front walls and foundation slabs. The two gun mounts were unserviceable but the barrels remained intact ... the concrete gun emplacement of the sixth gun bad been fired at by the battleship with 10 very heavy AP shells (44.5cm calibre) ... At the time of firing, a direct hit resulted in complete penetration of the shell through the emplacement ... It only exploded about 40 minutes later in the shelled terrain behind the emplacement. Consequently, it must have been fired with an adjustable delayed action fuse.'

Schmetzer's conclusions were:

'The four guns standing open without protective constructions withstood the numerous heavy bombing attacks far better than the concrete gun emplacements which the Führer had expected to have so much power of resistance. These emplacements were to be a standard type for guns of the most various types and calibres, immaterial whether they were used on gun carriages, so that they could be pulled out of the emplacement quickly to perform other tasks, or mounted on pivots as static guns. Their thick concrete protection was to assure the guns readiness for action even after the heaviest bombing attack or artillery fire They certainly did not fulfil their task. Their format, with the large embrasure, as well as their rear with the door, were particularly exposed to splinters, blast and shelling, also to the danger of bombs penetrating beneath the foundation. Since the lower edge of the structures was often only sunk into the ground two metres—or three metres at the utmost—and the walls at the front and rear also could not

Another view of Gatteville showing a typical open emplacement. The field gun was placed on a central mounting allowing the trail to move. This gave the gun a 360° traverse, unlike those limited by a casemate embrasure. NARA

Schmetzer's postwar report identified the 'tasks for the construction of concrete fortifications [in the invasion area] in sequence of urgency, were about the following:
a) Cherbourg was to be fortified, preferably with concrete constructions and with the main front toward the land.
b) At the same time, the east coast of Cotentin, which was particularly in danger of being invaded, was to be secured as much as possible, including St Vaast la Houge and an oblique line of defense on the flank along the Vire river upward.
c) The coast north and north-west of Caen, favourable for a landing operation, was to be fortified as well.
d) All coastal strips west of this area, from Caen to the mouth of the Vire river, along the so-called "signal peninsula" at the north-western corner of Cotentin, and at the northeast coast of the Norman peninsula, which were all suitable for secondary landings of enemy elements, were to be secured.
e) Development in depth was to be started in the nature of single concrete strongpoints as a framework for field-type fortifications along the east coast of Cotentin, in the area of Caen and on either side of this area to seal it off. The construction of concrete command posts, important observation, radio locating, and ranging stations, as well as of shore batteries in the area of Cherbourg, on the east coast of Cotentin, and in the area of Caen, was to be completed at the same time with equal constructions in the corresponding sectors.'

be adequately covered with earth, a protection of these two walls by means of protective walls, sunk to an appropriate depth had been demanded on principle. On account of the increased amount of work and material involved, the OT declined to carry out this reinforcement arguing that they could build more emplacements of this type in the short time available, which would be according to the Führer's intentions. Added to that was the impossibility to fit these high structures which towered over the terrain, unobtrusively into the ground or to camouflage them sufficiently. Without considerably increased forces, means, time and special installations which were no longer available owing to the circumstances ruling at the time, a solution could not be found to eliminate these serious weaknesses.'

In 1947, captured Generalleutnant Max Pemsel commented upon Schmetzer's report thus:

'A very accurate report by an expert for specialists on the question of the resistance capacity of the fortified defence installations. The heavy fortified defence installations of smaller size have proved their worth as shelters for men and ammunition and also as observation posts. As far as defensive installations were concerned, the little Tobruks were particularly popular.

'The large embrasures for guns have proved disadvantageous—as had been anticipated. Wherever the guns were not in embrasures but were well covered and camouflaged they remained undamaged for a long time. Their great advantage was that they offered only a small target, had a great mobility and were able to fire in all directions. Time, labour and material for the construction of the embrasures could have been saved. As the guns in the embrasures were to be as flexible as possible, the embrasures were too large and offered a good target to naval artillery. The more the embrasures were turned away from the sea, the greater the extent to which a wide field of fire was sacrificed.'

Why the Wall Failed

First and foremost, the failure of the Germans to repulse the Allied invasion did not just depend upon the strength of the defences which formed the Atlantic Wall. It also depended upon the strategic distribution of German forces within Northwest Europe. There were just under 60 divisions available in the west, but their strength, weaponry and fighting ability varied considerably: many of the infantry divisions being suitable only for local, static occupation use; others, such as FJR6, being better. In addition, only a few infantry and panzer divisions were up to anything like full strength, while many of the coastal divisions actually manning the wall contained an alarming number of what were described as 'Eastern Volunteers' whose combat abilities and loyalties were suspect.

We have already dealt with the rivalries, differences of opinion and of tactical concepts between the Heer and the Kriegsmarine, and also between various factions within both services; these were probably the most important factors which militated against a successful, unified command. The panzer controversy, for example, was a major expression of this internal squabbling and it was never resolved. This meant that there was never anything that could have been described as being a unified concept of defence on the Western Front.

As well as a shortage of forces, there was undoubtedly an acute shortage of weapons and equipment in all three services of the Wehrmacht. Almost everywhere there was a shortage of naval vessels, a shortage of fighter aircraft, a shortage of infantry weapons, a shortage of armour and artillery, and a shortage of mechanised troops, with too many horses still performing front-line duties. Despite the individual excellence of such basic items as the MG42, the MP40 submachine gun, and the Panzerfaust and Panzerschreck hand-held anti-tank weapons, they just could not compete with the overwhelming fire power of the Allies. It also did not help having a mixture of captured weapons in front line service, in particular artillery, which helped to complicate ammunition supply and led to ammunition shortages even for the 'sharp end' troops defending the beaches.

Equally important was lack of agreement at high level as to the most likely location for the coming invasion. Von Rundstedt and Rommel had for a long while generally agreed that the sector north of the Seine, in particular the area between Boulogne and Le Havre, was the most likely landing area. Nevertheless, the coastline of Normandy and Brittany was a close contender and became more likely as the days of spring 1944 lengthened into early summer. However, whilst they recognised this change, the German command did very little to alter the allocation of troops, or to take any real extra precautions. Even though Adolf Hitler had seen the Cotentin peninsula and the port of Cherbourg as becoming increasingly important, expressing this view at several meetings, little was actually done about it. These differences of opinion came to a head on 6 May, when von Rundstedt categorically turned down Rommel's requests to strengthen the Cotentin peninsula defences. Hitler's HQ supported Rommel, but in too half-hearted a manner, intimating that, whilst they agreed that the Cotentin could well be the first enemy objective, they could not agree that the western bay of the Seine had become the most probable landing area.

Other commanders also thought that the main landing area would be Normandy—these included General Erich Marcks, commander of LXXXIV Armeekorps, who would be in the thick of it when the invasion came.

The German View

It is interesting to read what has been written about the wall by senior Wehrmacht officers and Organisation Todt staff. Most of these views were written after the war, so are given with the benefit of hindsight and the knowledge that Hitler was safely under the sod. I doubt if they would ever have been brave enough to voice such defeatist opinions while the Führer was still alive. General der Infanterie Gunther Blumentritt, who was Chief of Staff OB West said:

'The Atlantic Wall was a propagandist's bluff, it was not as strong as was believed abroad. It was very strong on the coast of Holland and in the Fifteenth Armee sector on the Channel. However, the batteries of these mighty concrete works were silent when they were blanketed by pattern bombing and heavy naval artillery. The guns had only limited traverse; they were unable to fire to the rear on the land front. The ventilation (escape for gases caused by firing) did not function. The "wall" was a line, a chain of individual works without depth. If the enemy penetrated to a depth of one kilometre, they would be in free terrain. The installed guns were captured French, Belgian, Dutch, Polish, Russian and Yugoslavian materiel of all types and calibres with a variety of ammunition. Many had only a limited number of rounds available. Under heavy bombardment from the air and strong artillery fire from the sea. blanketed by smoke and attacked by airborne troops from the rear the "wall" could never have stopped an invasion. It was apparent that these concrete monsters were greatly overrated. We had to assume that these facts had been made known by the many foreign workers.'

Blumentritt goes on to explain just where the staff at OB West had considered the most probable invasion sites to be. 'The wide, jutting peninsulas of Normandy and Brittany' were one area considered, but discounted as it was thought that the route to Germany was too long from either of these locations. A landing in the Bay of Biscay in the First Army sector was possible, especially because there were 500km of coastline to be defended by just three divisions, of which two were composed mainly of recruits, but this site was just as far away. They considered diversionary

Intelligence
The brave spies who operated in all the occupied countries, often under the very noses of the Gestapo, played an important role in ensuring that the Allies knew as much as possible about the German defences prior to D-Day. Rene Duchet, a Caen house-painter, saw an announce-ment that the local OT was inviting bids from painters and decorators to refurbish its offices. His bid was purposely lower than anyone else's, and he was given the job. During his first interview with Gauleiter Hugo Schnedderer, Duchet was left on his own in the Gauleiter's office. He saw on the desk a map marked 'Special Blueprint—Top Secret'. He hid it behind a mirror and later retrieved it during his redecoration of the offices—helped by the fact that Schnedderer was posted elsewhere and the map was not missed. It was taken across the Channel by fishing boat and later arrived in London. After the war, then Commandant Duchet of the Deuxième Bureau was awarded the Medal of Freedom by the Americans (the highest honour a civilian can attain), whilst the French gave him not only the Medal of the Resistance but also the Croix de Guerre. Add to this the constant flow of informa-tion obtained from Ultra, air reconnaissance and all the other methods of gaining up-to-date facts and figures, and it is clear that intelligence played an important role in the planning stages of 'Over-lord' and thus in the Allied success. Furthermore, the mass of misinformation fed to the German intelligence ser-vices, typified by everything to do with Patton's mythical army group, waiting to strike at the Pas de Calais, also un-doubtedly played its part.

A German blockhouse in Langemark World War I cemetery outside Ypres. Hitler's view on fixed defences was informed by his time at the front in the Great war. German fixed locations are generally assumed to have been better than those of the Allies. They withstood massive artillery bombardments and allowed their occupants to emerge unscathed to repel an attack.

assaults on the Mediterranean coast to be a distinct possibility, but only to contain the German reserves. He comments that OKW, on several occasions, considered that landings might be made in Spain and/or Portugal, but OB West considered this even more unlikely for both political and military reasons—the terrain, the railways and roads were unsuitable; the Pyrenees would have to be crossed and 'the Spaniard fights well on his own soil'. After considering all these possibilities they went for the Fifteenth Army sector as being the most likely invasion location, between Calais and the mouth of the Seine He also had this to say about the level of support they had expected from the Luftwaffe and Kriegsmarine:

'The ratio of air strength between the Luftwaffe and the Allies on 6 June 1944 was 1:25. The Allies had not only air superiority, but complete mastery of the air, with all the obvious consequences for us. In the entire OB West area, the Navy had only 12 destroyers. I do not recall the number of E-boats. There was only a limited supply of naval mines. The Resistance movement in southern France was so strong that troop movements were delayed, communications were destroyed, and considerable casualties were sustained as the result of ambushes.'

General Franz Halder wrote in his pamphlet *Hitler as a General*:

'As a result of Hitler's distrust of the Heer officer corps he narrowed their field of employment more and more. This development begins with the assignment of fortification construction (the Westwall) to Todt ... After the Westwall, which nonetheless may have had a certain psychological importance at the beginning of the war although it was never of any strategic value, his [Hitler's] dictatorial order led to the construction of the Atlantic Wall, an over-sized construction project which caused serious damage to our forces in the east through its expenditure of labour and materials, without presenting any obstacle worthy of the name to the enemy invasion of 1944.'

Dorsch as one might expect, did not agree with these caustic comments:

'Aside from the fact that it is possible to hold a different opinion as to the psychological effectiveness of the Atlantic Wall and that at the time it was justifiable to assume that without the presence of the Atlantic Wall the invasion would have taken place considerably earlier, and precisely for this reason would have caused serious harm to the army fighting in the east at a considerably earlier time, and aside from the additonal fact that the opinion may be held that the value of a fortification can only be estimated in conjunction with an army which is still intact and not at a time when this army, for example, was admittedly handicapped with respect to its freedom of movement and striking power as the result of the almost complete failure of the Luftwaffe, there is the following to be said concerning Halder's statements:

'For the most part the construction of the Atlantic Wall was carried out at the same time as the construction of the submarine bases, various construction projects for the armament industry, repair work on destroyed railway installations etc. Altogether along with many other construction achievements, the OT poured somewhat more than 15 million cubic metres of concrete and reinforced concrete—to mention only one figure—in the occupied territories. With an overall personnel strength at the most important time of around 200,000 men on the job, approximately only 18,000 OT workers were employed; the average age of whom was about 55 at the end of the war! Even if the age of the OT's organic executive personnel and and that of its contracting firms, which had an average strength of 8,000 men, was substantially lower, it is nevertheless obvious that the deferment of men eligible for military service in the above-mentioned figures could not have

had a detrimental effect of any importance on the supply of manpower for the army fighting in the east, since, as already said, this figure included workers employed in the construction of submarine bases, who could by no means be dispensed with in view of the importance ascribed to these bases at that time. The construction of the submarine bases, itsclf was carried out at the same time as the construction of the Atlantic Wall, is mentioned because the conjunction of these two construction projects resulted in greater efficiency from the very beginning. Hitler's order in the summer of to speed up the completion of the Atlantic Wall could be acted upon so quickly because the five submarine bases were already employing a considerable number of construction workers, most of whom could be reassigned to the construction of the Atlantic Wall.'

Dorsch goes on in to justify the OT use of vehicles and supplies which could have been sent to the Eastern Front pointing out for example the more than half of the OT vehicles were rented from the French, Belgians and Dutch with their own indigenous drivers. Nor was the quantity of steel used in the Atlantic Wall of any importance to the overall military potential, especially since Speer had issued a special order for OT to use various kinds of iron which could not be used for armament purposes without special processing. Also, as he had already pointed out, only 24,000 of the 200,000 construction workers were actually Germans.

General Hans Speidel was more scathing about the OT than he was about the Atlantic Wall itself, although we have already seen how disappointed Rommel was when he carried out his first inspection. Speidel wrote in his book *We Defended Normandy*:

'The whole development of coastal defence, that is to say, the design and layout of the fortifcations, had been entrusted to an engineer of the Organisation Todt, who was neither tactically nor strategically proficient, had no knowledge of the general war situation and no experience of co-operation with the armed forces. There had been no chance of an agreed system of defences between the Heer, the Kriegsmarine and the OT, as between 1941 and 1943 the services had failed to agree upon basic principles.'

He goes on to explain how propaganda for the wall had begun in 1942. When the Dieppe raid had been beaten off, German propaganda had claimed a major success for the defences—in order to distract public from reverses on the Eastern Front, and OBW had 'regrettably associated itself with these optimistic claims. Goebbels had experience of "building-up" a defence line from the summer of 1938 when he put the Westwall of Germany on the map. Now he did the same for the Atlantic Wall. He picked on the strongest area, the "heavy offensive batteries group" at Cap Gris-Nez, and made it appear the whole of the Atlantic Wall was of equal strength.'

Being an entirely practical and pragmatic soldier, Rommel did not waste his breath complaining about the failure of the wall to stop the Allied landings, but rather expended his energies on fighting the battle in Normandy until his encounter with Allied fighter-bombers on 17 July. Because of his forced suicide on 13 October, we have no frank postwar assessment. However, from what he did mention in various battle reports after D-Day, we get the impression that he was entirely satisfied with the way the troops actually defending the wall had performed. For example, in a situation report written on 10 June, he said:

'As a result of the stubborn defence of the coast defence troops and the immediate counter-attacks launched by the available major reserve, the enemy attack, despite the strength of his effort, has gone considerably more slowly than he had hoped. The enemy also seems to be committing more forces than he had originally planned.'

Whatever the quality of the defences, the brunt of the Allied attack fell on the German infantry who did much to slow down the Allied advance in June and July 1944. Helped by the terrain — in the bocage it was easier to defend than to attack — the Germans bottled up the Allies, but they did so at a significant cost. Robert Kershaw assesses their casualties between 6 June and 31 August as being 288,875, 23,019 killed, 67,240 wounded and 198,616 missing or taken prisoner. The Allies' casualties were higher.

Elsewhere in the same report, when discussing the massive enemy use of heavy naval guns he comments:

'The effect is so immense that no operation of any kind is possible in the area commanded by this rapid-fire artillery, either by infantry or tanks. Yet, despite this heavy bombardment, the garrisons on the coast and the units who counter-attacked in the Montebourg area have held their positions with extreme stubborness.'

The Allied View

In his memoir *Crusade in Europe*, the Supreme Allied Commander, General Dwight D. Eisenhower, after explaining why the UK had been chosen as the main base for operations in Europe, goes on to say:

'From that point on we encountered the obstacle on which all discussions split and practically exploded in our faces. This was a very definite conviction, held by some of our experienced soldiers, sailors and airmen, that the fortified coast of Western Europe could not be successfully attacked. Already much was known of the tremendous effort the German was making to insure integrity of his Atlantic Wall. Moreover a considerable amount of the German Air Force could still be disposed in those areas and important elements of his fleet were lying in the harbours of northern France, in Norway and in the Baltic Sea. The coastline was crowded with U-boat nests, while undersea mining was rapidly covering every possible approach ... Many held that attack against this type of defence was madness, nothing but military suicide. Even among those who thought direct assault by land forges would eventually become necessary, the majority believed that definite signs of cracking German morale would have to appear before it would be practicable to attempt such an enterprise.'

Eisenhower explains that, fortunately, a few others took an opposite view and goes on to describe how they formulated a new concept, 'almost a new faith, to strategic thinking, one which envisaged the air co-operation with ground operations to the extent that a ground-air team would be developed. Tending to multiply the effectiveness of both.'

The plan to attack across the English Channel received President Roosevelt's blessing on 1 April 1942. Following the Casablanca conference of January 1943, it was decided to set up an Allied inter-service staff (COSSAC) to prepare a definite plan for Operation 'Overlord'. Winston Churchill, in volume V of his *History of the Second World War*, deals with the question of where the landing could be made:

'There were several options, the Dutch or Belgian coast, the Pas de Calais, between the mouths of the Somme and the Seine; Normandy, Brittany ... Normandy gave us the greatest hope. The defences were not so strong as in the Pas de Calais ... All the coast between Havre and Cherbourg was of course defended with concrete forts and pillboxes, but as there was no harbour capable of sustaining a large Army in this 50-mile half-moon of sandy beaches it was thought that the Germans would not assemble large forces in immediate support of the seafront ... If only there were harbours, which could nourish great armies, here was the front to strike.'

Churchill went on to explain how, as far back as May 1942, he had given the go-ahead to the building of the Mulberry Harbours, being a 'partisan of piers with their heads floating out in the sea'. Thus, whilst not discounting the strength of the Atlantic Wall, Churchill's fertile imagination had already found a major key to breaking into it.

What of the general who would command the initial landings—General Montgomery, who had been personally responsible for the simple, clear plan which eventually became the basis for 'Overlord'? He forecast that the fighting would be extremely hard, principally because Rommel was in charge of the Atlantic Wall. Monty's intelligence experts had rightly come to the conclusion that Rommel would try to defeat them as they came ashore, pushing forward his reserves, rather than assembling them to fight in depth. However, he appreciated that Rommel would need to commit his armour. As Monty's biographer Nigel Hamilton says:

'By personalising the enemy as "Rommel", he (Montgomery) was able to clarify and simplify the scenario—alerting all to the sense of contest between opposing wills: "Since Rommel toured the Atlantic Wall the enemy has been stiffening up his coastal crust, generally strengthening his defences and redistributing his armoured reserve. The present trend of movement of his mobile reserves is South—i.e. away from the 'Neptune' ('Overlord') area; this shows that our target is not yet known to the enemy. Rommel is likely to hold his mobile Divisions back from the coast until he is certain where our main effort is being made. He will then concentrate them quickly and strike a hard blow; his static Divisions will endeavour to hold on defensively to important ground and act as pivots to the counter-attacks ... Some of us here know Rommel well. He is a determined commander and likes to hurl his armour into the battle ... but according to what we know of the chain of command, armoured divisions are being kept directly under Rundstedt and delay may be caused before they are released to Rommel."'

How different things might have been if Rommel had actually had control over Geyr von Schweppenburgs Panzer Group West and had been able to move it freely from the outset without the continual threat from Allied air superiority.

General Omar N. Bradley views were:

'Unable to anticipate where we might strike, the enemy had been forced to spread his strength across 860 miles of European coastline. As he continued to plant more German dead on his long line of retreat from Russia, it became increasingly difficult for him to man the Atlantic Wall. To smash our way ashore we had only to concentrate a force against some single point in his line. With the firepower at our disposal we could break a hole in that line and pour our follow-up forces through it.'

Bradley then went on to affirm that the Atlantic Wall would never have halted an intruder, but that it could, and did, slow down an attacking force whilst reserves were summoned to counter-attack. In other words, it was there to:

'Blunt our assault and so split our forces so that the form his reserves and strike enemy might find time to form his reserves and strike back in counter-attack. When used to screen a mobile reserve in this fashion, the concrete fortifications of a fixed defensive line can be worth many divisions. Without these mobile reserves, however; a fixed defensive line becomes useless.'

This is the most telling argument as to why the Atlantic Wall failed. Fortunately, it would appear that Hitler thought somewhat differently—he said after talking to one of the workmen who built the wall: 'a man hates to abandon such safe positions as those on the Channel coast, captured during the campaign in France and consolidated by Organisation Todt.' Fortunately he either did not remember the words of Frederick the Great or chose to ignore them. 'He who defends all defends nothing'—perhaps that would be the most fitting epitaph for Hitler's Atlantic Wall.

Rommel inspects the Normandy beaches in January 1944. Sucked into a battle of attrition without airpower, there was little he could do once the Allies had won the race to get reinforcements onto the bridgehead. And while the battle was raging in Normandy, garrisons in the other occupied countries could do little but await their fate. J.P. Benamou Collection

CREDITS

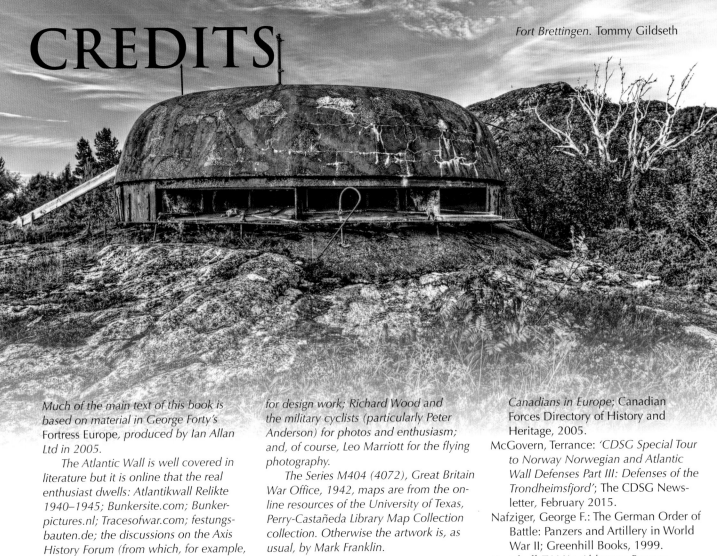

Fort Brettingen. Tommy Gildseth

Much of the main text of this book is based on material in George Forty's *Fortress Europe,* produced by Ian Allan Ltd in 2005.

The Atlantic Wall is well covered in literature but it is online that the real enthusiast dwells: *Atlantikwall Relikte 1940–1945; Bunkersite.com; Bunkerpictures.nl; Tracesofwar.com; festungsbauten.de;* the discussions on the Axis History Forum (from which, for example, the info on AR1716 on p77 comes)— the huge base of knowledge available through these sites beggars belief. On top of this, organisations such as the Dutch Stichting Bunkerbehoud who are restoring and preserving structures should be mentioned (and congratulated).

The many photos in this book come from a number of sources. Grateful thanks go to *BattlefieldHistorian.com,* NARA College Park, MD, and the George Forty Library for historic photos; to Thierry Llansades of La Rochelle for material on the French Atlantic coast; to Kurt Lund Mogensen for the splendid contemporary Danish material; to Tommy Gildseth for much of the contemporary and historic Norwegian material; to Petr Podebradsky for his superb Norwegian material; to Richard Quist of the Atlantikwall-Museum, Stichting Vesting Hoek van Holland; to Lenco van der Weel of Stichting Bunkerbehoud for help with Walcheren material; and to Raphael Smid of www.bunkerpictures.nl for Dutch and other images. Other credits are noted on the photographs—WikiCommons has proved extremely useful. If anyone is missing or incorrectly credited, apologies: please notify the author through the publishers.

Other thanks are due to Jonathan Forty for scanning and preparation; Elly

for design work; Richard Wood and the military cyclists (particularly Peter Anderson) for photos and enthusiasm; and, of course, Leo Marriott for the flying photography.

The Series M404 (4072), Great Britain War Office, 1942, maps are from the online resources of the University of Texas, Perry-Castañeda Library Map Collection collection. Otherwise the artwork is, as usual, by Mark Franklin.

Bibliography

Most of the research material for the book came from the online sources mentioned above. Other sources include:

Andersen, Jens: *The Atlantic Wall – from Agger to Bulberg;* Blåvandshuk Egnmuseum, 1999.

After the Battle: magazines and books.

Bernages, George: *Omaha Beach;* Heimdal, 2011.

Beyer, Dr John C. and Schneider, Dr Stephen A.: *Forced Labor Under the Third Reich, Part One and Two;* Nathan Associates Inc.

Ebert, Vibeke B.: *The Atlantic Wall from Nymindegab to Skallingen;* Blåvandshuk Egnmuseum, 1992.

Harrison, Gordon A.: *US Army in World War II The European Theater of Operations Cross-Channel Attack;* CMH Washington, 1993.

Jervas, Bjorn: *German coastal defence in Norway during WW II;* www.feldgrau.com.

Maass, Walter B.: *The Netherlands at War 1940–45;* Abelard-Schuman, 1970.

Matti, Ernest W. [trans]: *World War II Invasion of Normandy 1944 Interrogation of GenLt Rudolf Schmetzer;* Naval History and Heritage Command.

McAndrew, Bill, Rawling, Bill, and Whitby, Michael: *Liberation: The Canadians in Europe;* Canadian Forces Directory of History and Heritage, 2005.

McGovern, Terrance: 'CDSG Special Tour to Norway Norwegian and Atlantic Wall Defenses Part III: Defenses of the Trondheimsfjord'; The CDSG Newsletter, February 2015.

Nafziger, George F.: The German Order of Battle: Panzers and Artillery in World War II; Greenhill Books, 1999.

Pantcheff, T.H.X.: *Alderney, Fortress Island;* Phillimore & Co Ltd, 2005.

Rolf, Rudi, and Saal, Peter: *Fortress Europe;* Airlife Publishing Ltd, 1988.

Saunders, Anthony: *Hitler's Atlantic Wall;* Sutton Publishing, 2001.

Short, Neil: *Tank Turret Fortifications;* The Crowood Press, 2006.

Stacey, Col. C.P.: *Official History of the Canadian Army in the Second World War V III The Victory Campaign The Operations in North-West Europe 1944–1945;* Ottawa, 1966.

Speidel, Hans: *We Defended Normandy;* Herbert Jenkins, 1951.

US Army Training Manual TM-E 30-541.

Williams, Paul: *Hitler's Atlantic Wall: Normandy: Construction and Destruction;* Pen & Sword, 2013.

Zaloga, Stephen: *Cherbourg 1944;* Osprey Publishing, 2015.

Fortress The Atlantic Wall (1): France; Osprey Publishing, 2007.

Fortress The Atlantic Wall (2): Belgium, the Netherlands, Denmark and Norway; Osprey Publishing, 2009.